The *Perfect* *Blend*

A Practical Guide
to Designing Student-Centered
Learning Experiences

MICHELE EATON

International Society for Technology in Education
PORTLAND, OREGON • ARLINGTON, VIRGINIA

The Perfect Blend

A Practical Guide for Designing Student-Centered Learning Experiences

Michele Eaton

© 2020 International Society for Technology in Education

Senior Director of Books and Journals: Colin Murcray

Senior Acquisitions Editor: Valerie Witte

Development and Copy Editor: Linda Laflamme

Proofreader: Lisa Hein

Indexer: Valerie Haynes Perry

Book Design and Production: Danielle Foster

Cover Design: Edwin Ouellette

Library of Congress Cataloging-in-Publication Data

Names: Eaton, Michele, 1986- author.
Title: The perfect blend : a practical guide to designing student-centered
    learning experiences / Michele Eaton.
Description: First edition. | Portland, Oregon : International Society for
    Technology in Education, 2020. | Includes bibliographical references and
    index.
Identifiers: LCCN 2020006290 (print) | LCCN 2020006291 (ebook) | ISBN
    9781564848451 (paperback) | ISBN 9781564848437 (epub) | ISBN
    9781564848420 (mobi) | ISBN 9781564848444 (pdf)
Subjects: LCSH: Blended learning. | Student-centered learning.
Classification: LCC LB1028.5 .E274 2020 (print) | LCC LB1028.5 (ebook) |
    DDC 371.33/4--dc23
LC record available at https://lccn.loc.gov/2020006290
LC ebook record available at https://lccn.loc.gov/2020006291

First Edition
ISBN: 978-1-56484-845-1
Ebook version available

Printed in the United States of America
ISTE® is a registered trademark of the International Society for Technology in Education.

About ISTE

The International Society for Technology in Education (ISTE) is a nonprofit organization that works with the global education community to accelerate the use of technology to solve tough problems and inspire innovation. Our worldwide network believes in the potential technology holds to transform teaching and learning.

ISTE sets a bold vision for education transformation through the ISTE Standards, a framework for students, educators, administrators, coaches and computer science educators to rethink education and create innovative learning environments. ISTE hosts the annual ISTE Conference & Expo, one of the world's most influential edtech events. The organization's professional learning offerings include online courses, professional networks, year-round academies, peer-reviewed journals and other publications. ISTE is also the leading publisher of books focused on technology in education. For more information or to become an ISTE member, visit iste.org. Subscribe to ISTE's YouTube channel and connect with ISTE on Twitter, Facebook and LinkedIn.

Related ISTE Titles

Dive Into UDL: Immersive Practices to Develop Expert Learners
Kendra Grant and Luis Perez

The New Assistive Tech: Make Learning Awesome for All!
Christopher R. Bugaj

To see all books available from ISTE, please visit iste.org/books.

About the Author

 Michele Eaton has a passion for high-quality online and blended learning, both for students and adults. As Director of Virtual and Blended Learning for the Metropolitan School District of Wayne Township in Indianapolis, Indiana, Michele provides support for the Achieve Virtual Education Academy teachers and students, oversees online course design throughout the district, and helps to lead the district's many blended learning options. She started her career as a second-grade teacher but has also taught online for IUPUI (Indiana University Purdue University Indianapolis) in both its Learning by Design master's program and undergraduate education program.

Michele is a Certified Education Technology Leader (CETL) and was recently named a NextGeneration Leader by EdScoop and the Consortium of School Networking (CoSN). She was also selected as a 2018 Education Week Leader to Learn From and a 2019 ISTE Making IT Happen award winner. Michele currently serves as President for the ISTE Online and Blended Learning Network and as a conference chairperson for ISTE's Indiana affiliate organization (Indiana Connected Educators).

Continue the conversation beyond the pages of this book by connecting with her (@micheeaton) on Twitter or using the hashtag #PerfectBlendBook. You can also follow along as she helps moderate the #INeLearn chat on Thursday nights at 9 p.m. ET.

Publisher's Acknowledgments

ISTE gratefully acknowledges the contributions of the following:

ISTE Standards Reviewers

Suzanne Becking

Melissa Fierro

Billy Krakower

Colleen Skiles

Peer Reviewers

Diana McGhee

Tracey Knerr

Contents

PART 2: THE DIGITAL CLASSROOM

Foreword

At the time of this publication, we are in the midst of a pandemic, prompting educators to find innovative ways to teach their students from home. While staying at home during this time is difficult for all of us, consider what it means to be a teacher working at home with children who have their own needs. Teachers want to make a difference—that's the reason most of us went into the profession in the first place. It's important to remember as we deal with this changing world what's most important: to foster relationships.

Building a culture of learning is based on trust and respect that starts with the relationships between the teacher and students. An effective teacher:

- empowers students to be a designer of their own learning

- helps students gain confidence in their abilities to acquire new skills

- shows students what it means to be invested in their success

This personalized learning approach is about focusing on students as learners and empowering agency so they have choice and a voice in their learning. Many teachers believe that providing a set of pre-planned choices may be enough to give students opportunities for choice. Actually, providing choice in this way means teachers are doing most of the preparation and planning. In designing with student agency in mind, Michele Eaton shares how to provide choice in assessment by providing options with the tools students use to demonstrate what they learn. The idea of developing opportunities for choice is to start turning over these decisions to students so they can drive their own learning.

To achieve true student agency, providing opportunities for choice is not enough. Students need a real voice in their education. Students have more flexibility at home to work online with individualized content at their own pace while having more control over time and place.

Michele defines blended learning as any combination of traditional instruction and online learning. Because of the newfound need to stay at home, teachers are becoming more creative in using collaborative tools. There are more instances of blended learning via video conferencing using tools like Zoom, Skype, Microsoft Meeting, and Google Meet. You will also see students self-advocating for their learning at home and as a partner in learning with teachers. They will self-reflect on their learning journey and who they are as a learner by creating and monitoring their learner profile. The teacher uses a Flex Model with checklists, playlists, choice boards, and formative assessment strategies to encourage voice and choice. Videoconferencing creates an environment where you can listen and see each student more than when you are in a traditional classroom. You may find yourself spending more time building those relationships online using humor, games, and creative student-to-student interactivity.

Because students are in the comfort of their homes with parents more involved in the learning process, the relationships between the teacher and the families become stronger. You can even have one-to-one conversations using videoconferencing, email, or phone. When you first start reaching out to your students, you may make mistakes, and that's OK. If you build a culture of learning where everyone cares about each other, you will see that your online environment encourages vulnerability and supports social-emotional learning.

The Perfect Blend provides the blueprint as you grow as a blended learning educator. It lays out ideas on how technology allows teachers to restructure their classroom in a way that puts an emphasis on student-centered learning, data-driven decision-making, and individualized instruction. It offers the perfect blend of theory around agency, voice, choice, flexible approaches, accessibility, and using digital tools. When your students take more control of the path, pace, time, and place for their learning at home, you will find yourself developing more agency designing new content in new ways. I know you will enjoy the activities, stories, and resources found in each chapter to be invaluable as you rethink your role as a partner in learning with your students and their families. I invite you to read through this book rethinking your WHY as a blended learning educator.

Barbara Bray, Creative Learning Strategist, Podcast Host, Author of *Define Your Why*
Oakland, California

Introduction

Do you want to leverage technology to improve the teaching and learning in your classroom? Are you unsure where to start? Are you looking for a way to meet the needs of a diverse group of students with various strengths and needs? Blended learning could be the solution for your classroom. *The Perfect Blend: A Practical Guide to Designing Student-Centered Learning Experiences* can help you redesign your lessons to use technology in ways that help you individualize and personalize instruction for students. Let's move away from using technology for the sake of technology, and instead let's use it to transform what learning looks like in your classroom.

What's in This Book

Blended learning in its simplest form is any combination of face-to-face instruction and online learning. This book is divided into two parts to cover those two components.

Part 1, "The Physical Classroom," explores the elements of the traditional classroom that impact the blended learning experience. You will learn about blended learning models and structures that you can adapt, reflect on the role of student agency, and make a plan for data collection to drive instruction. We will also discuss strategies for designing an active learning space in which student-centered blended learning can take place, as well as for classroom management in such a modern learning environment.

Blended learning relies on high-quality online instruction to be effective. Part 2, "The Digital Classroom," examines the components of high-quality online learning. After addressing the differences between learning online and more traditional instruction, it shares digital teaching strategies that will help you make the most of the online environment. You will learn ways to immediately improve the digital content that you deliver to students, as well as how to create equitable and accessible digital learning opportunities that meet the needs of all students.

Throughout the book, you will find several recurring elements to help you on your blended learning journey. Every chapter includes an opening list of learning objectives to guide your reading, a section outlining the corresponding ISTE standards covered, QR codes and links to additional templates and resources, a summary of the chapter, and reflection questions to think about independently or as part of a book study.

Whom This Book Is For

This book is for teachers and teacher leaders who want to make a change in their classrooms. Although some incredible blended schools and programs required major planning and shifts at a high level, they are not the only model. You do not have to wait to be placed in a blended school; you can get started personalizing and individualizing instruction in your own classroom tomorrow. That's right—regardless of the school or system in which you teach, this book will help you implement blended learning for your students. If you are not satisfied with a one-size-fits-all approach to education, then The Perfect Blend is the perfect resource to effect change.

As you read and reflect, I hope you will join me on Twitter, Instagram, or your social media platform of choice using the hashtag #PerfectBlendBook. Share your thoughts, questions, ideas, and favorite resources with our community.

Happy blending,

Michele (@micheeaton)

PART 1

||||||||||||||||||||||||||||||||||||||||

The Physical Classroom

CHAPTER 1

Understanding Blended Learning for Your Classroom

By the end of this chapter, you will:

- Understand what blended learning is and its impacts on traditional instruction

- Understand the differences between differentiation and personalization and blended learning's role in facilitating these types of learning experiences

- Start to view yourself as an architect of learning in the modern classroom, embracing the flexibility of blended learning

- Understand the theory- and research-based rationale for incorporating blended learning in your classroom

ISTE Standards

This chapter addresses several ISTE Standards for Educators.

1. Learner

   Educators continually improve their practice by learning from and with others and exploring proven and promising practices that leverage technology to improve student learning. Educators:

   a. Set professional learning goals to explore and apply pedagogical approaches made possible by technology and reflect on their effectiveness.

5. Designer

   Educators design authentic, learner-driven activities and environments that recognize and accommodate learner variability. Educators:

   a. Use technology to create, adapt and personalize learning experiences that foster independent learning and accommodate learner differences and needs.

6. Facilitator

   Educators facilitate learning with technology to support student achievement of the 2016 ISTE Standards for Students. Educators:

   b. Manage the use of technology and student learning strategies in digital platforms, virtual environments, hands-on makerspaces or in the field.

What Is Blended Learning?

Maybe you have heard the term *blended learning* and gathered it refers to a strategy for integrating technology in your classroom. But what does that really involve? Simply put, blended learning is any combination of face-to-face, traditional instruction and online learning. The online learning portion, however, does not mean simply integrating technology into your classroom. For instance, using such collaborative tools as Google Docs or Microsoft OneNote, videoconferencing with students around the world, and introducing your students to online games to enhance learning are all great examples of integrating technology into the modern classroom, but not of online learning. For the purposes of this book, online learning as a part of the blended classroom specifically means digital content, instruction, and assessment being delivered as part of the learning for students.

Multiple Ways to Blend a Classroom

That is a fairly vague definition, isn't it? The incredible thing about blended learning is its flexibility. Blended learning can look different based on your individual classroom, school, and students. I like to think about blended learning as a spectrum (Figure 1.1), with completely face-to-face, traditional classrooms on one end and online classes for distance learners on the other end. Any combination of the two along this spectrum would be blended learning.

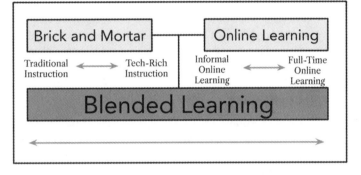

1.1 Blended learning happens on a spectrum. It is any combination of online learning and traditional instruction. Some blended classrooms use a lot of online learning, relying heavily on it, and others use just a little online instruction.

All along this spectrum are formally defined models of blended learning (Figure 1.2), ranging from minimal to extensive use of online learning. If you are interested in learning the specifics of these models as defined by the Clayton Christensen Institute, check out the "Models of Blended Learning" sidebar.

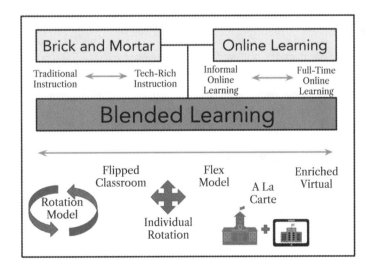

1.2 There are multiple formal models of blended learning that fall along the blended learning spectrum.

5

Models of Blended Learning

A leader in blended and personalized learning research, the nonprofit Clayton Christensen Institute focuses on the tools and strategies necessary to solve problems we face in the modern classroom. In research studying the various ways blended learning was being implemented around the country, for example, the Clayton Christensen Institute found that most blended classrooms follow one of seven models (Horn & Staker, 2014). Although a basic understanding of these models and the various ways you can blend your classroom is important, don't become bogged down trying to replicate any specific model exactly. Feel free to embrace the flexibility of blended learning and to combine pieces of the models described below with your own ideas to create the *perfect blend* for your students.

Station Rotation

The Station Rotation Model is one that will feel familiar to many elementary school teachers. In this model, the teacher sets up stations for groups of students to move through during class time. The teacher determines the group members and time spent at each station. The number of stations that students move through can vary. Generally, at least one station should be devoted to small group instruction with the classroom teacher. A teacher can incorporate online learning into one of the stations. Students can do partner and group work, projects, or other offline activities at the remaining stations.

Lab Rotation

The Lab Rotation Model incorporates traditional, face-to-face classroom instruction with online instruction that happens in a lab. Students move on a teacher-determined schedule. At least one of the stops on a student's schedule is a computer lab. In the computer lab, students can work on online learning. In many examples of a Lab Rotation Model, paraprofessional staff members help facilitate the lab, while certified staff provide instruction in other classrooms.

Students move from classroom to classroom receiving face-to-face instruction and online instruction in the computer lab. This model is similar to the Station Rotation Model, with the primary difference being in the physical location of the learning.

Individual Rotation

Another model that is similar to the Station Rotation Model, the Individual Rotation Model once again features stations, one of which features online learning. However, in this model, students do not move with a set group of peers. They each have an individual, personalized schedule. Students move to different stations on a set schedule, but they may not go to all of the stations. This is a highly personalized experience for the students that requires a great deal of planning on the part of the teacher if technology is not available to automate this scheduling.

One of the greatest benefits of this model is the customization based specifically on student needs. Unlike the previous models, students do not have to go through every modality for every lesson. They get exactly the kind of instruction they need at exactly the right time (Reading Horizons, 2019).

Flipped Classroom

The Flipped Classroom Model is based on the concept of flipped learning, one of the first forms of blended learning that became popular in traditional classrooms. The basic premise of flipped learning is that online learning is used as a homework tool, freeing up the teacher during class time to help with student application. The online learning portion of the instruction could be as simple as a video lecture that students watch at home. Students could work through more sophisticated online lessons at home as well.

Online learning is used in this instance as a way to make the best use of the teacher's classroom instruction time. In a traditional model, homework is how students get dedicated time to practice a skill. The inherent problem with this is the absence of the teacher when a student does not fully understand. In the worst-case scenario, students practice something the wrong way, making it even more difficult for them to eventually master the skill.

Under the Flipped Classroom Model, instead of spending class time providing basic instruction, teachers are able to essentially replicate themselves. The teacher moves the basic instruction online in a carefully crafted assignment and is "present" when the student is learning at home. The teacher then dedicates subsequent in-class time to helping students apply that learning, avoiding the homework practice dilemma.

Flex

The Flex Model of blended learning is very similar to the Individual Rotation Model with two main differences: Online learning plays a heavier role in the Flex Model, and the teacher's role in this environment is different as well. The teacher provides much of the instruction online and creates offline supports for the students.

continues ▶

▶ *continued*

According to the Clayton Christensen Institute (2019), "the Flex Model lets students move on fluid schedules among learning activities according to their needs." Additionally, students have a greater amount of control in this particular environment. Many classrooms using the Flex Model look more like neighborhood coffee shops than traditional classroom spaces, with flexible seating to replicate the student choice that is a part of this model.

A La Carte

The A La Carte Model uses online learning in a much different capacity. Instead of integrating traditional instruction with online instruction within the same course, this type of model blends a student's schedule. A school or district can offer individual courses online to supplement a student's course schedule at a brick-and-mortar school. Some classes can be taken completely online, and others are taken completely face-to-face.

Enriched Virtual

The Enriched Virtual Model uses online learning as the primary vehicle for instructional delivery. This method of instruction allows the students to complete the majority of their work outside of a traditional brick-and-mortar setting. Because it is still a blended learning model and not fully online, students are asked to come for face-to-face learning sessions at specific times. Online learning is the primary mode of learning, and the face-to-face opportunities in a brick-and-mortar setting supplement that learning.

Generally speaking, when programs or classrooms are created with a large percentage of online learning incorporated, as on the right side of Figure 1.1's blended learning spectrum, these are innovative solutions created for alternate student populations. Districts and schools around the world are creating opportunities for students that create multiple pathways to success, especially for those learners who are not finding the success they could in a traditional setting. In these situations, online learning can be used strategically to give students the greatest amount of flexibility, allowing learners to engage with their classwork at their own pace and sometimes outside of a traditional school building with a teacher facilitating that instruction in a self-paced environment.

Blended learning also has a place in classrooms where students are finding success and with students for whom a traditional setting is a good fit. In these settings, however, it is best to stick to blended learning on the left side of the spectrum. Online instruction and assessment paired together is one tool that can help amplify and enhance learning in a classroom. In a traditional classroom, moving students through full online courses at their own pace is often not a necessary strategy or the best use of the teacher in a brick-and-mortar setting. The good news is the forms of blended learning that make sense for most general classrooms can usually be implemented within your classroom, regardless of the structure of your school or district and within the constraints of an established curriculum and mandated standards.

Designing the Perfect Blend

Although the Clayton Christensen Institute defines seven specific models, I have found that there is more fluidity in most classrooms, enabling you to be creative with your implementation. You may find that you move from one model to the next throughout your day or year. You might also find yourself creating hybrids of these different types of blended learning in ways that do not fit a formal definition. That is okay! The goal for implementation should never be to exactly replicate a model of blended learning that is working somewhere else. So much depends on your own teaching style; the constraints of your particular school, district, or state; the lesson or subject you are teaching; and the unique students in your classroom. Ultimately, a solution that is very successful for one classroom may be a poor fit for another classroom's teacher and students.

ARNETT ARTICLE

The other thing to keep in mind as you design your perfect blend is that it is not about the technology. Software, online lessons, and devices cannot improve learning on their own. A highly effective teacher is still the most important aspect of any classroom. The technology simply allows you to restructure your classroom in a way that puts an emphasis on student-centered learning, data-driven decision-making, and individualized instruction—all of which are possible only with a skilled teacher. Thomas Arnett (2018) wrote about this in his article "The Secret Element in Blended Learning" (**bit.ly/ secretelement**), exploring John Hattie's Visible Learning study, which ranked educational practices associated with academic achievement. Focusing on those practices specifically related to blended learning, Arnett found that although technology can have a positive impact on the classroom, the largest effect sizes show up when we are able to shift instructional practices. Technology becomes the lever that makes that work possible.

As you navigate this book, don't expect a ready-made recipe for perfectly implementing an existing model of blended learning. Instead, you will be given a road map for finding your own perfect blend. We will examine the various components of blended learning to help you determine the characteristics that make the most sense for you, your students, and the content you want to teach. Determining the blended learning components that work best for you may be a process of trial, error, and refinement. My own journey to the perfect blend was not a smooth trip, but it may serve to help ease yours.

My Story

Believe it or not, I did not start out as an incredibly "techy" teacher. I have always enjoyed using technology in my personal life, but when it came to my first teaching assignment, I was a fairly traditional second-grade teacher. Like many elementary school teachers, I used small group instruction as an important part of our literacy block. I felt strongly that this was essential to growing readers and writers. I worked hard to create independent work that would keep my students engaged and quiet while I worked with small groups. I created beautiful laminated station activities and file folder games. My students also each had their own journal for their reading response activities. My learners would do independent or partner reading and then answer prompts in their personal journals.

A Crate of Good Intentions

Although I felt good about the instruction happening at my little kidney table with those small reading groups, I soon became dissatisfied with the independent work during our reading block. I'm embarrassed to admit this, but my metric for success in that environment was compliance and not learning. Students were quiet, were on task, and appeared to be engaged in the activities. The problem was I didn't feel like learning was happening in this space. It was practice at best. At worst, it involved students practicing skills incorrectly without me really knowing how they were doing. I was measuring success by the noise volume in the room, the students' attention to their tasks, and honestly, the "cute factor" of my laminated activities. This was not good enough for my learners. I wanted to provide instruction for *all* students in my class, not just the five or six in my small group.

While I am describing my early shortcomings, let me tell you about those reading response journals. Almost daily that first semester, I wheeled home my materials crate filled with a stack of reading response journals with the plan of providing handwritten feedback in them for my students. Let's be real, that's what it *looked* like. Turns out, I had a million other things to worry about as a teacher, and the journals became less of a priority in my evenings. As the year went on, the facade even dropped; I wheeled home that crate of journals less and less—and it showed in more ways than one. As the year went on, my students became better readers and writers, but the quality of their reading response entries steadily decreased. The students figured out fairly quickly that I was the only person reading their work, and even that was not happening frequently. Their work did not matter, and their effort reflected that. The compliance I saw in my classroom was fake engagement.

My students deserved better. I wanted to do something different.

The Power of an Expanded Audience

Enter some student devices. As a first step, I changed the environment for the reading response activities to a digital discussion board. I started this transition with some mini-lessons on sharing in a digital environment and writing constructive comments. Students learned about leaving helpful feedback for their friends that moved beyond basic "I like what you wrote" statements. Then an amazing thing happened.

By simply moving this work to a digital space, the quality of work I saw from my second graders began to skyrocket. I had given my students an audience. It may not have been global or revolutionary, but it was someone to write for, peers that were invested in interacting with their work. All of a sudden, the work mattered again. Plus, the feedback on the writing was no longer my sole responsibility. The students were keeping each other accountable, learning how to give helpful peer feedback.

The other benefit that I quickly noticed, which was the spark that ignited my love of blended learning, was my changing role in this independent activity. Before, I was limited in my ability to teach during the stations because I was always with a small group of students. Leaving handwritten feedback in the reading response notebooks was equally inefficient because of the time it took to find each student's latest entry and then write out my thoughts. I found I could type or record feedback a lot faster than I could write, and with the discussion board, all of their responses were in the same place. More importantly, I started to take advantage of that digital feedback to actually teach. I was able to ask my students questions, give them additional prompts to address when they got back to class, and share resources to expand their understanding. I no longer had to be physically next to students to teach them. My teaching may have happened at 9 p.m. at home or during my in-school prep period, but the metric for success of student independent work time was no longer compliance. I knew how my students were doing, and I could take an active role in their learning.

Growing Our Role

That was the lightbulb moment for me. When I saw the benefit of simply moving this kind of activity into a digital environment, I began to realize that I could create online lessons for my students. I could create opportunities for instruction and assessment, and then use the data I received from those digital lessons to guide the face-to-face instruction in our classroom. Essentially, incorporating online learning into my second-grade classroom gave me the ability to "clone" myself. When I used technology to free up the time, place, and pace of learning, my role as a teacher grew, and the learning experiences in my classroom were richer. A small change made a big difference for me, and it can for you too.

The Research

Although I feel strongly from my own personal experiences that blended learning has the potential to make a positive impact on teaching and learning in the classroom, there is more than just anecdotal evidence to support this practice.

Blended learning is no silver bullet, and it can be implemented poorly. However, when carried out with efficacy and an intentional focus on improving instruction, it can lead to incredible academic achievement. Here are some links to research and case studies that bear witness:

 **Blended Learning Success Case Studies.** The Clayton Christensen Institute partnered with the Evergreen Education Group to publish twelve case studies of traditional school districts that experienced improved academic performance with the implementation of blended learning. I recommend checking out these case studies, as they follow

school districts around the country with varied demographics, approaches, and goals. You can find links to each in the article "Proof Points: Blended Learning Success in School Districts" available at **bit.ly /proofpts** or by scanning the QR code.

Blended Learning Universe. The Blended Learning Universe website (**blendedlearning.org/research**) has an extensive repository of research around blended learning, along with other design tools to help you as you begin to implement online learning into your classroom.

Clayton Christensen Institute. The Clayton Christensen Institute's focus on disruptive innovation has led to a great deal of research on the power of blended learning. The Institute's website (**bit.ly/CCIresearch**) houses hundreds of examples of blended and personalized learning research done around the world.

The Learning Accelerator: Blended & Personalized Learning at Work. The Learning Accelerator is a nonprofit organization that focuses on innovation in the classroom. Its Blended & Personalized Learning at Work website (**bit.ly/LAblended**) has several tools and resources to help teachers understand how to implement personalization and competency-based learning in their classrooms. One powerful portion of the website includes several profiles of schools across the United States and their particular strategies for innovating in the classroom. This is a great website to explore to find examples of blended learning in action.

Chapter 1 Key Points

In this section, the important takeaways from the chapter are paired with the ISTE Standards for Educators that inform them.

- Blended learning is any combination of face-to-face, traditional instruction and online learning (specifically online instruction and assessment, not just using technology). (Educator 1a, 6b)

- Blended learning cannot be designed with a one-size-fits-all approach. We can vary the amounts and ways we use online learning to accomplish specific goals in the classroom. It should be very personal and unique to you and your students. (Educator 1a, 5a)

- Blended learning is a great strategy to help you get the most out of small group or individualized instruction. (Educator 5a, 6b)

- Restructuring your classroom with online learning can allow you to "clone" yourself by creating opportunities for instruction beyond the confines of the four walls of the classroom. (Educator 1a, 6b)

Reflection

After reading Chapter 1, take some time to consider how its ideas apply within your context using the questions below.

- What is your "why" for investigating blended learning?

- What problems could you solve by incorporating online learning in your classroom?

- Explore some of the links shared. Was there a school or classroom example that resonated with you? Why?

Share your reflections and thoughts online using the hashtag #PerfectBlendBook.

CHAPTER 2

Designing with Student Agency in Mind

By the end of this chapter, you will:

- Understand the differences between differentiation and personalization

- Understand blended learning's role in facilitating personalized learning

- View aspects of student agency in terms of path, pace, time, and place as they design a blended learning structure

- Gain ideas for encouraging student agency in the classroom

- Know the importance of academic and affectual data to foster student success and engagement

ISTE Standards

This chapter addresses several ISTE Standards for Educators.

1. Learner

   Educators continually improve their practice by learning from and with others and exploring proven and promising practices that leverage technology to improve student learning. Educators:

   c. Stay current with research that supports improved student learning outcomes, including findings from the learning sciences.

5. Designer

   Educators design authentic, learner-driven activities and environments that recognize and accommodate learner variability. Educators:

   a Use technology to create, adapt and personalize learning experiences that foster independent learning and accommodate learner differences and needs.

6. Facilitator

   Educators facilitate learning with technology to support student achievement of the 2016 ISTE Standards for Students. Educators:

   a. Foster a culture where students take ownership of their learning goals and outcomes in both independent and group settings.

7. Analyst

   Educators understand and use data to drive their instruction and support students in achieving their learning goals. Educators:

   a. Provide alternative ways for students to demonstrate competency and reflect on their learning using technology.

   c. Use assessment data to guide progress and communicate with students, parents and education stakeholders to build student self-direction.

Personalized Learning in the Blended Classroom

Let's be clear from the beginning: Simply adding a component of online learning into your classroom will *not* guarantee the transformation of your students' classroom experience. That said, however, you will see one component in almost all successful blended learning implementations. You will see student agency.

Student agency is present when learning is meaningful, relevant, and driven by a student's personal interests. Students who have true ownership of their learning take an active role in their education by experiencing opportunities for voice and choice in the classroom. Students, not the teacher, are the center of the classroom, each deciding what they are going to learn, how they are going to learn it, and/or how they can demonstrate mastery of what they have learned.

Blended learning creates an environment that allows students some autonomy over their learning. By personalizing the learning experience, we can increase student engagement, provide workable and manageable solutions to individualize learning, and help students learn what it means to be successful self-regulators. In turn, we also help increase student agency.

You would be hard-pressed to find a teacher who does not believe in the basic premise of personalized learning, the belief that helping students take ownership of their learning has a positive effect on the students' classroom experience. There might be disagreements on various approaches or implementations, but ultimately, we all want to help students develop into lifelong learners that can identify and solve problems.

It is not an issue of whether teachers want this for the classroom. The reality is that it is hard to wrap our heads around what personalized learning looks like in a full classroom of students with diverse strengths and needs, a strict state- or district-mandated curriculum, and an already substantial workload placed on the teacher. Additionally, if you are trying to achieve more than very basic differentiation in lessons without expensive adaptive software, it can feel almost insurmountable.

I am here to tell you that we can break down and implement personalized learning in a way that is realistic and feasible for the modern classroom. You can do it with adaptive software, or you can do it in an environment with access to just a few devices and completely teacher-created content. The important thing to remember is what is at the heart of personalized learning: students. It is not about going 1:1 or devices or expensive software. Personalization is about creating a student-centered learning environment.

In almost any discussion of student agency and personalized learning, someone will eventually mention differentiation. Although the terms *personalization* and *differentiation* are often used interchangeably, they actually represent two very different types of instruction. I like to think about one key difference, and that is who is in charge of changes made to a learning activity. In differentiation, the teacher makes adjustments and changes in the learning activity to help a student be successful. In personalized learning, students make adjustments and changes in the learning activity to help themselves be successful.

To take that one step further, blended learning is not necessarily personalized, and vice versa. However, the two can (and I think should) go hand in hand. Blended learning can be the environment that makes personalization possible and effective. We can design blended experiences with student agency in mind.

I am not advocating that we get rid of differentiation, however. We should all be slow to discard strategies and structures that work in exchange for the latest and greatest buzzword. Finding the appropriate time to differentiate while finding ways for students to have some autonomy in those decisions is all part of the art of teaching. As you will learn in Chapters 3 and 4, some aspects of blended learning can lend themselves to creating opportunities for differentiation, while others are more suited for personalization.

Voice and Choice

The simplest way to think about student agency or personalized learning is to consider how we are giving students opportunities for voice and choice. A personalized environment will allow students options for how they learn material and demonstrate mastery. It also will give students a voice in what their learning looks like.

Choice

Choice is often a good first step to creating opportunities for student agency in the classroom. It is a very important first step, too. We know a lot about the importance of choice, not only in education but also in our day-to-day lives.

Some interesting consumer research exists about choice and shopping habits, which offers a lot of parallels with our blended classrooms. In his 2013 research on purchasing decisions, Daniel Mochon found that choice is incredibly important and identified a tendency he called "one-choice aversion." Imagine going to the store to look for a particular item. If you get to the store and there are no choices, just one product available, even if that particular product is the best on the market or the most highly rated option of the item you are looking for, you are subconsciously more likely to still hate that product. This is simply because you do not have a choice (Mochon, 2013).

Consider how this applies to our own classrooms. Even with those subjects that we view as very interesting and naturally engaging for students, what happens when we don't give students a choice in learning that content? Is it possible that when we teach these lessons and hand-select every piece of content or map out exactly how a student demonstrates mastery, we are encouraging students to dislike or disengage with the lesson? Are we fueling one-choice aversion? To some extent, I would argue that it is not enough to even create incredible assessments or projects. It is not enough to find the highest-quality interactive content to create beautiful, interactive digital content. By not giving the students any choice, even the best lesson ever written could be received poorly by students because they were not given a choice.

How can we provide students more academic choices? Students can have choices in how they learn content, and they can be given a choice in how they are assessed over that content. You can incorporate both these opportunities for choices effectively in online lessons used during blended learning.

Choice in Learning Material

Consider a scenario for giving choice in how students learn the material. Imagine you are designing some digital content with options for how students receive direct instruction. The students access the direct instruction and are given three choices for the instructional content: a video, a text-based resource, and an interactive simulation or slides. The students are given the directive to choose two of the three pieces of content. When the students get to the assessment, it is helpful to add in a reflection question where the students share which two resources they selected and why. That piece of information does two things for you. It helps you collect some data about the types of content your students are drawn to. It also helps you reteach more successfully.

Choice in Assessment

Imagine a student goes through that lesson and struggles on the assessment. For the purposes of this example, let's say the student selected the text-based resource and the interactive slides as the content for the lesson. One of the benefits of blended learning is how it can make differentiation and remediation more efficient. If you wanted to help this student and provide another opportunity to demonstrate mastery, another text-based resource would not make sense. If the student read the text and was not successful on the assessment, offering more of the same would not be the most reliable method to reteach. If, instead, you had built varied reteaching materials into the lesson already, you could direct the student to watch the video content they did not choose at the beginning of the lesson. This provides additional materials to help the student review the content without creating extra work for you. Plus, those reteaching materials are in a different medium than what the student initially accessed.

This leads to creating options for assessments. Certainly, we can give students options in the tools they use for different assessments. If we give an option for what the assessment looks like, that also creates a built-in option for remediation. If a student is given a chance to retake an assessment, relying on the exact same quiz or assessment is not the most accurate way to determine if the student has reached proficiency. Has the student reached mastery or merely remembered or reviewed the answers from the first time they took the assessment? However, if you previously had given students the choice of multiple assessment types, you can give a student a second, different assessment after getting some extra instruction without any additional planning effort on your part.

Balancing One-Choice Aversion and Paralysis of Mind

When designing choice-filled lessons, beware of providing too much of a good thing. Having too many choices can be just as detrimental as having only one. In 2000, researchers Sheena Iyengar and Mark Lepper found that too many options can prevent us from successfully making a choice. Researchers presented shoppers with a table with twenty-four varieties of jam, then later with another table holding only six kinds of jam, The study found that the table with more options created more interest from shoppers, but ultimately more sales were made from the table with fewer options. The researchers found that because vast numbers of variations create a "paralysis of the mind," it was difficult for consumers to choose the best option (Iyengar & Lepper, 2000).

So what does this mean for our blended classrooms? While we know that providing choices for our students is critical, we must strive for a balance. Too many choices can make it difficult for students to adequately and efficiently make a decision. Part of a teacher's critical role is to provide choice in a structured way.

Unfortunately, I do not have quantitative guidelines about what this balance looks like. It will vary based on your students and their unique needs. As you design digital content, remember the jam shoppers' dilemma. There is a clear difference between giving students a small number of varied ways to access the material versus a comprehensive list of all possible resources. Likewise, there's a difference between creating a few assessment options for students and leaving it vague and wide open for all students to demonstrate mastery in whatever way makes sense to them. As you design these experiences for students, be mindful about striking this balance.

Voice

If the goal is to achieve true student agency, providing opportunities for choice is not enough. We must give students a real voice in their education. This means students have input on the classroom and their learning. They are empowered to shape their own learning, which moves the instruction to a truly student-centered approach.

Connie Scalzetti's fifth-grade class at Chicago International Charter School (CICS) West Belden is a good example of enabling students to shape their own learning. Instead of using the common "exit ticket" approach in which students fill out a quick formative assessment just before leaving class, Connie has students complete an "entrance ticket," a pre-assessment for the day's learning that the students then check themselves. After taking a look at their data, students decide whether they are going to "Seminar," which is direct instruction with the teacher (Figure 2.1), or if they are going to "Workshop." Workshop has several options for the students to extend their learning with real-world application and hands-on work both independently and collaboratively.

By incorporating online learning into a personalized model of instruction such as Connie's, you could bring blended learning together with voice and choice. Part of the teacher's role as architect of learning in this environment is to consider structured voice and choice and to be on the lookout for students feeling overwhelmed. Often, creating opportunities for true student agency in the classroom will require scaffolding. For most students, we have trained them in what Robert Fried called the "game of school" (2005): how to be successful in a model that views them as a container that educators must pour knowledge into. Giving students control over their education could be a new experience for your learners, and we must teach them what it means to advocate for themselves as learners.

2.1   Connie Scalzetti teaching in her fifth-grade classroom

Pace, Path, Time, and Place

Blending your classroom can create opportunities for student agency and voice over four aspects of your students' learning:

- Pace
- Path
- Time
- Place

One of the scariest things about personalizing learning, whether it is in a blended classroom or not, is the fear of losing control, but your classroom does not need to turn into the "wild, wild west" to give students a voice. At any given time, students do not need to have agency over pace, path, time, *and* place. For example, in a math class, it may be more difficult to give students much control over the path of their learning. You can give them choices in how they learn the content, but each topic and lesson might have to be completely controlled by the teacher. In a math class, often each lesson builds on itself, creating a foundation for the next lesson. In this environment, you may put more focus on student agency in the pace of learning to help ensure each student is reaching mastery before moving on to the next concept. A student-centered learning environment does not mean a lack of structure.

What you give students control over in your classroom is a personal decision. It depends so much on what you are teaching, the time of the year (especially for our youngest learners), your teaching style, and the individual students in your classroom. It can change from semester to semester, day to day, and even lesson to lesson. Although students do not have to drive every decision in the classroom, you should be designing experiences that allow them to be in the driver's seat for some aspects of each lesson. As the year progresses, also consider how that student agency is growing or changing and adapt your lessons to accommodate your students' increased mastery.

Technology is more than a tool to entertain or engage students. It can be the vehicle for truly personalized learning that empowers students to take ownership of their learning. As you will see in the following sections, technology can play a vital role in improving student agency in pace, path, time, and place.

Pace

In a traditional classroom setting, pacing of a lesson is based on the teacher who works hard to differentiate and remediate to help all students find success. This is a difficult task, and the truth is, when the date for the end of the lesson arrives, everyone moves on to the next lesson, regardless of levels of mastery. A consequence of a teacher-paced lesson is that it creates a perpetual problem: When a student does not quite reach mastery of a particular topic, the student starts the next lesson with a disadvantage. Every time a student has to move on without fully understanding the material, a hole is created in the foundation of their learning. These gaps make it difficult to be successful with subsequent content, especially in subjects with content that builds on itself, such as math. It is not difficult to see how that creates an environment where students start the year behind and end the year behind as well.

Blended learning can give students more flexibility in the pace at which they move through the content. For example, by strategically adding online learning throughout a class or even a lesson, you can give students control over the pace at which they complete their work and ultimately reach mastery. Such blended learning also allows for more instructional time in the classroom, giving you important data that can drive the face-to-face instruction.

LINDSAY HIGH SCHOOL

With its highly personalized approach to English and English language learning, for example, California's Lindsay High School provides students with agency over the pace at which they move through their learning (The Learning Accelerator, n.d.). Students can work across grade levels using playlists at their own pace during specifically designated self-directed learning time. This self-paced work ensures that learning is mastery-based and not based on a fixed amount of time. While students are able to work through content at their own pace, Lindsay High School still expects students to work through and master a certain amount of content each year. Students who are off-pace receive multiple supports to get caught up, including designated time during the day for personalized learning with direct support from teachers, detailed pacing guides and matrixes, and student choice over their own personal mastery level (whether they want to achieve proficiency or a more advanced level of mastery). For more information about Lindsay High School's approach, visit **bit.ly/LHSpace**.

Flexible pacing does not perfectly solve the difficulties of helping all students reach proficiency in every lesson if you are still working within a traditional classroom or strict curriculum. However, blended learning does create a manageable environment that makes the work more feasible.

Path

Incorporating online learning into your daily classroom routine can also facilitate individualized learning in a more manageable way by giving students some agency over the path of their learning. When some of the instruction happens online, students can make decisions about how they learn the material and what assessments they complete.

The path of learning can be individualized for students even without giving them the agency over those decisions. Adaptive software and programs can be wonderful tools for providing digital content that meets students exactly where they are and moves them to the next step in their learning in a competency-based fashion. Many of these programs are labeled as "personalized," but teachers should be wary. Tools like these can be incredibly powerful additions to the classroom, but I urge you to consider where students get to demonstrate agency in a blended environment heavily reliant on adaptive software. Although adaptive software can provide highly individualized instruction, if not used intentionally, it can suppress the very agency it professes to encourage. If students have no control over the path of their learning, it is teacher- or computer-driven and not student-centered.

Although personalized paths throughout a lesson can be accomplished without technology, a blended learning environment has the potential to make the process of personalizing learning paths more manageable, freeing you to focus on using data received from students' self-directed learning to create individualized and differentiated learning experiences for students.

PLEASANT VIEW ELEMENTARY

Fifth-grade teachers at Pleasant View Elementary in Providence, Rhode Island, for example, facilitate personalized and blended learning in their classrooms by leveraging student agency over path (The Learning Accelerator, n.d.). Students in these classrooms begin each unit with a pre-assessment. This pre-assessment helps the students identify their levels of proficiency over the learning objectives. Students then take this information to make decisions about playlists, resources, and supports they need to be successful and reach mastery. Because this is a big responsibility for elementary students, the teachers scaffold support for students, gradually releasing the responsibility to the students. For more information about Pleasant View's approach to personalized learning, visit **bit.ly/PVESpath**.

Online instruction within a blended classroom gives a teacher the tools they need to do what technology cannot. In Chapter 4, we will do a deep dive into specific strategies and tools to help students gain more autonomy over the path of their learning.

Time and Place

Finally, a blended learning environment allows students to gain some control over the time and place of their learning. When we move some instruction online, students are no longer bound by the four walls of the classroom. We, as teachers, can remove ourselves as the sole agent of knowledge in the classroom. Students can continue learning any place and at any time—and teachers can provide instruction at any time. As I shared in Chapter 1, incorporating online lessons into the structure of the school day meant that I could continue teaching even if I was at home. All I needed was my laptop or phone and access to the digital learning environment where some of my instruction was housed.

We will take a closer look at tools to provide students control over pace, path, time, or place in Chapters 3 and 4. For now, take some time to consider what a good first step might be for your particular students. In what areas are you wanting to give students more autonomy? What aspects of your classroom currently require the most structure to help your students be successful?

Student Data and Self-Reflection

For true student-centered learning to be possible, students must learn to reflect on their own data, both academic and non-academic. This includes assessment data, information about their mastery of various learning objectives, and their own soft skills acquisition. To make decisions about their learning, they have to understand where they are and where they are going. This is a journey, and the following chapters offer several ideas to help you embed those self-reflective learning opportunities into your day-to-day instruction. In the meantime, let's take a closer look at the role of data in the design of our blended learning lessons.

Data-Driven Decision-Making

It is also important for the teacher to use data to drive learning and to keep a pulse on student engagement. Keep in mind that regardless of the blended learning model you design, it will be critical for you to connect the learning that happens both offline and online. Research from Garrison and Kanuka (2004), Garrison and Vaughan (2008), and Gerbic (2006) tells us it is important for the learning in the digital space and the physical space to be deeply integrated. If both the online learning and face-to-face instruction are isolated from each other, you are not likely to see many academic gains. So, for example, if you have students working through some software that is individualized and adaptive while you meet with small groups, it is still not likely that you will see major academic gains in your students if you are not using the data from that online learning—either information provided by the adaptive software or from your observations—to drive the instruction happening elsewhere in the classroom. However, when both the online and offline learning are connected and the data from each is used to individualize instruction for students, that is when blended learning is transformational.

The data you are able to gather will vary based on your online learning solution. For most of the classrooms in my school district, that means taking a look at student performance on digital tasks that the teachers have designed themselves. If you are using a learning management system, check out the kinds of reports you can run on various assessments. They may provide useful insights or simple statistics; the reports you can pull from software will vary in sophistication as well. The most important thing is to have an understanding of how students are doing in their self-directed learning and to craft your instruction and small groups accordingly.

Measuring Engagement

It is not just academic data that matters either. We know from several research studies, some from as early as 1968, that student engagement has a direct correlation with academic success. Fostering engagement, as mentioned earlier, does not mean merely keeping students entertained, but rather keeping them deeply invested in their learning. This affectual data is just as important to track as the data that shows progress toward mastery.

MEASURE WHAT MATTERS

STUDENT ENGAGEMENT TOOLKIT

Chris Young (@ChrisYoungEDU), Strategic Learning Coordinator for the Community School Corporation of Southern Hancock, understands the importance of measuring what matters. To help you track engagement, he created the Student Engagement Toolkit. As Chris explained (2020), "We measure nearly everything else in education—from student grades, assessment data, attendance, and more. How are we measuring interest in our lessons? Are students engaged? In real time, are they even understanding the content?" The Student Engagement Toolkit gives teachers a resource to help answer these questions in real time during a lesson (Figure 2.2). It works with the Plickers app (**get.plickers.com**), and you can download it from **bit.ly/measuremyclass**. To hear from Chris directly, scan the QR code to check out his video "Measuring What Matters" (**bit.ly/CYmeasure**).

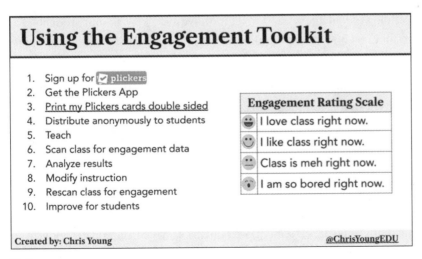

2.2 Instructions from Chris Young's Student Engagement Toolkit

Learner Profiles

Part of becoming a self-advocate for your education involves understanding yourself as a learner. In their book *How to Personalize Learning* (2016), Barbara Bray (@bbray27) and Kathleen McClaskey (@khmmc) shared ideas for developing learner profiles for students. These learner profiles were checklists of descriptors designed to help students self-identify their strengths, needs, and interests. Students would fill out these checklists and then write summaries about what they learned about themselves.

**LEARNER
PROFILE TOOL**

Since the release of their book, Bray has worked with teachers who have adapted the original Learner Profile Tool to use in their own classrooms. Based on feedback and more research, she recently updated the Learner Profile Tool to reflect Universal Design for Learning (UDL) and a student's "why" for learning (Bray, 2019). You can find this new Learner Profile Tool at **bit.ly/BBlearnerprofile** (or scan the QR code).

Self-Regulation

Now, I know what you might be thinking: "What if my kids just are not ready for all this ownership? What if they just can't handle it?"

Remember, you can start small. Students do not need control over everything in the classroom. It is okay to scaffold student agency and to let it evolve and grow as your students learn. If you do not teach them how to self-regulate and take responsibility for their learning and their work, how will they learn it?

Self-regulation is all about making the decisions that are in our best interest, even when those decisions are not as desirable as others. It is a critical life skill. It is also a key reason we are successful adults. Because I am a good self-regulator, I show up to work on time. I go to meetings that I do not always want to attend. It is also the reason I choose not to eat cupcakes for breakfast every day. They might be delicious, and no one is here to tell me that I can't, but I know it is not best for me.

If you have ever witnessed kids with a big bag of trick-or-treat candy after Halloween, you know most are not inherently good at self-regulation. For that same reason, you cannot wait to start giving students some control over their learning until they are "ready" for it. We have to help them become ready. There will be times that you have to repeat yourself, provide multiple mini-lessons, and sometimes remind that same student over and over what it means to make a good decision about their learning. It will not always feel easy, but it is important to do it anyway. We have an awesome responsibility and opportunity to help students become self-driven learners, facing a future of jobs that do not yet exist to solve problems that will need creative solutions. To do that, we must first teach them to self-regulate, engage with learning they are passionate about, set goals, and track their progress toward those goals.

Chapter 2 Key Points

In this section, the important takeaways from the chapter are paired with the ISTE Standards for Educators that inform them.

- One component of a successful blended learning implementation is student agency. (Educator 5a, 6a)

- Student agency is present when learning is meaningful, relevant, and driven by a student's personal interests. We often think about it as "voice and choice." (Educator 5a, 6a, 7a)

- In differentiation, the teacher makes adjustments and changes in the learning activity to help a student be successful. In personalized learning, the students make adjustments and changes in the learning activity to help themselves be successful. (Educator 5a, 6a, 7a)

- Giving students choices in the learning is critically important. However, those choices should be structured so students do not feel overwhelmed. (Educator 1c, 5a, 6a, 7a)

- Students should be given a voice in their learning. Student agency can be experienced when students have control over the pace, path, time, or place of their learning. (Educator 5a, 6a, 7a)

- A successful blended learning classroom is heavily reliant on data, about both academic achievement and engagement. We must teach students to use their data to make good decisions about their learning. (Educator 6a, 7c)

Reflection

After reading Chapter 2, take some time to consider how its ideas apply within your context using the questions below.

- Did you have any misconceptions about student agency or personalized learning? Has your thinking changed since reading this chapter?

- What aspects of your classroom instruction are truly personalized? In what areas would you like to give students more agency?

- Consider your current group of students and a typical semester. What aspects of student agency make sense throughout the day or the semester? Where can you give students control over pace, path, time, or place of learning?

- In what ways might you measure engagement and self-regulatory skills in students?

Share your reflections and thoughts online using the hashtag #PerfectBlendBook.

Differentiation and Your Blended Classroom

By the end of this chapter, you will:

- Understand the basic characteristics of the Station Rotation Model, including some iterations or variations of the model
- Gain ideas for differentiation using station rotation
- Explore ideas and templates for stations that could be incorporated into the classroom
- Have the tools necessary to plan a station rotation lesson or unit

ISTE Standards

This chapter addresses several ISTE Standards for Educators.

3. Citizen

   Educators inspire students to positively contribute to and responsibly participate in the digital world. Educators:

   a. Create experiences for learners to make positive, socially responsible contributions and exhibit empathetic behavior online that build relationships and community.

5. Designer

   Educators design authentic, learner-driven activities and environments that recognize and accommodate learner variability. Educators:

   a. Use technology to create, adapt and personalize learning experiences that foster independent learning and accommodate learner differences and needs.

   b. Design authentic learning activities that align with content area standards and use digital tools and resources to maximize active, deep learning.

   c. Explore and apply instructional design principles to create innovative digital learning environments that engage and support learning.

6. Facilitator

   Educators facilitate learning with technology to support student achievement of the 2016 ISTE Standards for Students. Educators:

   a. Foster a culture where students take ownership of their learning goals and outcomes in both independent and group settings.

   b. Manage the use of technology and student learning strategies in digital platforms, virtual environments, hands-on makerspaces or in the field.

The Basics of the Station Rotation Model

A good first step for many teachers when getting started with blended learning is the Station Rotation Model. Students move through stations in teacher-developed groups for set periods of time (Figure 3.1). One of those stations should be small group instruction, and one of the stations should include some form of online learning.

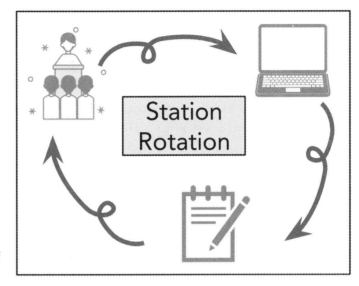

3.1 A three-station example of the Station Rotation Model

Many teachers are comfortable with running stations as part of their day-to-day instruction. If that describes you, then you are just one small step away from blended learning. In fact, you may actually be doing blended learning already without even knowing it!

The reason this form of blended learning is a good entry point into blending your classroom is because of the level of control and structure the teacher provides. Although the Station Rotation Model of blended learning is not inherently personalized, as the locus of control is with the teacher, it can be great for differentiating instruction, which may be just what your classroom needs. The model also serves as a useful stepping-stone to becoming more comfortable implementing increased student voice and choice into the structure of your lessons.

Choosing the Number of Stations

To organize a station rotation setup in your classroom, you first need to decide how many stations to create. The answer is completely a matter of personal preference. So much depends on what tasks need to be accomplished, how large you want the group sizes to be, how long each station should be, and so on. You can have as few as two or as many as you want. Because one of the stations should involve small group instruction, however, consider how many students you want in that face-to-face teaching time. If you divide your class into groups of that size, you can determine how many stations you need to enable you to optimize that time.

Timing of Each Station

Each group will move through the stations together. The teacher determines who is in each group, at which station they start, how long they stay at that station, and when to move on to the next station. The class moves on a schedule determined by the teacher. How long you have students stay at a station before rotating to the next one is completely up to you. One strategy for determining how long each station should last would be to divide the available class time by the number of stations that you have. You would need to adjust each station accordingly to make sure that enough time is allotted to adequately complete each task.

You are not limited to just one class period or day to work through stations, however. Remember, there are no hard rules for doing blended learning correctly if you are using online learning in intentional ways to improve instruction in the classroom. If you need a longer timeframe to be able to get through a meaningful small group instruction period or to complete a digital lesson, then feel free to spread out stations over a couple of days. It could even take a week to move through all of the stations. That's okay!

Regardless of how long you make each station, the important thing to plan for is meaningful small group instruction and time spent outside of that small group *learning* and not simply completing busywork. Figure out how much time you need to accomplish that, and then figure out a schedule that makes sense for your students.

Setting Up Groups

Dividing your class into their station groups is a great opportunity to differentiate. Because as the teacher you set the pace and activities in this form of blended learning, you can individualize activities per group. You can choose to have all students do the same learning activity at each station or you can create specific tasks and lessons that are unique to different groups.

If you're grouping students to differentiate, I highly encourage you to do so using flexible ability grouping as opposed to static ability grouping or tracking. Professor Steve Higgins and colleagues from Durham University (2012) compiled a teaching toolkit summarizing a variety of research. In this toolkit, they shared that tracking of students in class or between classes can often have no impact or even a negative impact on students, specifically those who are from low socioeconomic backgrounds or are below grade level. Higgins and his team found that static ability grouping led to lower expectations for students, less effort

Finding the Perfect Blend for Station Rotation

Diane Johnson, a fifth-grade teacher at Lawrence E. Boone Elementary School, is a great example of a teacher who evolved her blended learning practice to be very individualized for her classroom. As she reflected on the needs of her students, the structure of her station rotation began to shift to become the "perfect blend" for her particular class.

JOHNSON'S ROTATION APPROACH

Diane began blending her classroom using a three-station version of the Station Rotation Model. During this time, she would pull small groups for additional support. She wanted more autonomy for her students, so she began to modify the Station Rotation Model, giving her students more freedom. After a few iterations, Diane found that she was able to provide some flexibility and student ownership of the learning, while retaining some of the structure of a more traditional station rotation. For more details about how Diane modified the Station Rotation Model, check out Jenny White's article "Flexibility in an Elementary Classroom" at **bit.ly/DJstationrotation**.

As you read about the evolution of Diane's classroom, consider what aspects of the Station Rotation Model would work well in your classroom and what updates you would need to make.

from students because of an interpretation that achievement is fixed and cannot change, and self-esteem issues from identifying as part of a low-achieving group.

Instead, creating opportunities for fluid, flexible grouping can have a positive effect on learning. Kelly Puzio and Glenn Colby (2010) conducted a meta-analysis on in-class flexible grouping. They found that in reading instruction with truly flexible groups, students were able to make great progress and growth. The key is to avoid making permanent or semi-permanent groups. Creating groups that are skill-based instead of overall performance-based is a good start. Through constant assessment, groups should change from one lesson to the next. A blended environment gives you lots of data to make that happen, from both the small group instruction and the assessment data from the online instruction.

If students are grouped by proficiency, each station can have different tiered tasks based on the students' unique needs. You can label tasks at each station by the group name or number, giving you a lot of control over differentiating for each group.

Sometimes it may not make sense to group by ability. You may choose to group students heterogeneously to ensure high expectations are maintained for all students and to give students the opportunity to learn from each other. You could also group students by interest if that makes sense for the topic. Depending on your class and your comfort with it, there is no reason why you should not let students pick their own groups occasionally, too. When grouping students in this way, I encourage you to consider incorporating aspects of personalization. Give students opportunities to reflect on their learning and make choices at some or all of the stations.

Variations of the Station Rotation Model

In addition to spreading out stations over multiple days, there are a few ways you can iterate on the traditional model of station rotation. Give yourself the freedom to make adjustments that work best for you and your students.

Different Station Lengths

One way to alter the Station Rotation Model is to plan stations without uniform time lengths. You can organize your stations to still function on a schedule without all stations being the same amount of time.

For example, if you had a three-station rotation, one station could be long and the other two stations could be half that time. Imagine that you have an hour of time to work with for your stations. You could do one thirty-minute station and two fifteen-minute stations. You can accomplish this by dividing the class into two groups. One group would go to the thirty-minute station (maybe that's the instruction with the teacher or the online learning portion). The other group would be split into two sub-groups and go to the two fifteen-minute stations. After fifteen minutes, those two groups would switch, while the larger group kept working. After thirty minutes, the two smaller groups would come together for the larger station, and the other group would split into two sub-groups (Figure 3.2).

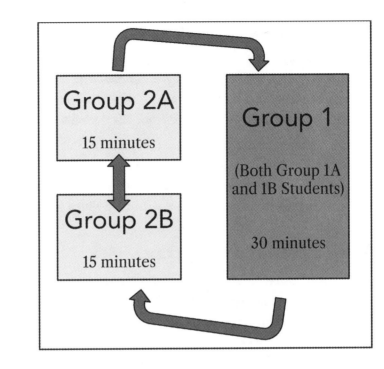

3.2 One example of how you could create stations of differing lengths

Student-Paced Stations

You might find that with a traditional implementation of the Station Rotation Model, the amount of time needed to complete each task varies for each student. You can address this with differentiation or additional activities, or you can adjust the timed nature of your stations.

If the timed stations are not giving your students the flexibility and freedom that you would like, you can move to student-paced stations. In this version, instead of setting a timer and having all students move at the same time, students would move on to the next station when they complete their work at the current station.

Clear expectations would need to be set about how to transition from one station to the next without disrupting others who are working. You also will need to be extra cognizant of the opportunities for collaboration if students are moving at their own pace. We do not want to sacrifice collaborative learning opportunities for the sake of implementing a certain kind of blended learning.

One Station Each Day

If you find that you want students to spend more focused time on each station, you have the option of spreading out stations, one per day. With a three-station setup, for instance, students would move to a different one for three days. This strategy gives the students more time at each station and cuts down on time lost during transitions.

Instead of making small group instruction a station, this iteration of the Station Rotation Model gives you a lot of flexibility in pulling groups. In other words, you could pull students from their stations to form a small group. These students would not have to all be from the same group if you do not make the time with a teacher a scheduled rotation.

Varied Stations Each Day

Keep in mind that if you choose to design a station rotation structure for your class or one of the subjects that you teach, you are not bound to the same stations each day. You could design the number of stations, station types, or role of the teacher by day. For example, the first day of your week may be dedicated to whole group instruction with no blended learning. You might also want to dedicate one specific day to student goal setting or student conferencing.

I encourage you to consider the needs of your particular classroom and not feel trapped into a type of blended learning that is so structured you can't adapt it. One idea would be to start with a structured, maybe even traditional, Station Rotation Model. Once you are comfortable with that and see what works and what doesn't work in your classroom, you could start making adjustments that make sense for your students.

Regardless of the way you implement the Station Rotation Model, remember to make it your own. If you have the flexibility of another co-teacher or paraprofessional in the room, it is okay to use them to get rid of the rigidity of this model as well. It is perfectly fine to pull students for tutoring or support if the fixed time is not serving them.

Planning for a Station Rotation Lesson

After you decide how many groups and stations you want to incorporate into a station rotation, it's time to start planning the blended lesson. As you are reflecting on the activities to incorporate, I encourage you to consider how students will participate in them. How many stations do you want to be online versus offline? Collaborative versus independent? Active versus stationary?

Station Ideas

So what should students do at stations where they are not working directly with the teacher or working on their online learning? Table 3.1 offers some ideas for learning stations you could incorporate into a blended learning classroom, and many of them easily can be done without technology. Remember, the goal of blended learning is not necessarily to have students in front of a screen all day. The digital learning is just a component of the overall strategy. (We will discuss how to create engaging and effective online learning in Part 2 of the book.)

Table 3.1 Learning Station Inspiration

STATION IDEA	TOOLS/STRATEGIES
Listening/Recording	• Audiobooks • Podcasts • Flipgrid.com
Discussion	• Offline discussions with conversation cards • Discussion boards
Writing	• Online collaborative documents (Google Docs, Microsoft Word Online) • Pre-writing graphic organizers • StoryboardThat.com
Active Reading	• Reading response • Annotation using online collaborative documents (copy text into a document and use the highlighting and commenting tools to annotate it) • Note-taking
Vocabulary	• Graphic organizers • Quizlet.com
Design/Makerspace	• John Spencer's Maker Challenges for Students (bit.ly/JSmaker) • Passion projects
Review Previous Material	• Review games and activities • Spiral review or practice
Scavenger Hunts and Active Learning	• QR code scavenger hunt (try the QR Treasure Hunt Generator at classtools.net/QR) • Digital breakouts (breakoutedu.com/digital)
Book Clubs	• Novel studies in groups
Research	• Research projects • Student presentations

Because of the independent nature of stations, it is also important to include clear directions at each station. This is especially critical if you do not have additional adult help in the classroom during your stations time. Consider if your instructions will be text-based, online or offline, or recorded in some way. Even if you go through the instructions as a whole class before moving into stations, it's a good idea to have the instructions clearly listed at each individual station for students' reference.

**STATION ROTATION
PLANNING TOOL**

To help you design your blended lesson using the Station Rotation Model, you can use the lesson-planning template shown in Figure 3.3. It can also help you ensure that you are balancing the types of learning activities you are having students complete at each station. To download a copy, scan the QR code or go to **bit.ly/PBstationplan**.

3.3 The Station Rotation Planning Tool can help you design blended lessons with a balance of learning activities.

Lesson

Date(s):	Topic:	Learning Objectives:

Groups

Group 1:	Group 2:	Group 3:	Group 4:

Stations

Station Activity and Resources	Instructions (To be printed or posted online)	Modality	Interaction
Station 1:		☐ Online ☐ Offline	☐ Individual ☐ Partners ☐ Small Group
Station 2:		☐ Online ☐ Offline	☐ Individual ☐ Partners ☐ Small Group
Station 3:		☐ Online ☐ Offline	☐ Individual ☐ Partners ☐ Small Group
Station 4:		☐ Online ☐ Offline	☐ Individual ☐ Partners ☐ Small Group

The Perfect Blend   @micheeaton   (cc) ① ⓪

Planning for Collaboration and Interaction

One of the most important parts of the Station Rotation Planning Tool, in my opinion, is the Interaction column. Interaction is something that can be easily overlooked when designing blended experiences, regardless of the model you choose to use, as the following story demonstrates.

Experience versus Observation

At a virtual and blended learning conference a few years ago, a principal of a middle school shared his school's story of transforming to a completely blended model. As the principal was doing his walk-throughs, he became very excited about the on-task behavior and engagement he saw in so many classrooms. One room especially impressed him. The teacher was leading a small, flexible group of students through an engaging lesson. Each student in the room was working through an individualized online learning lesson. The students were all working on content unique to them and moving at their own pace. Every single student in the class was on task, seemed engaged with learning, and was working at just their right level.

The principal was so proud! He took photos and immediately emailed the consultants he had been working with to share his observations and to thank them. The response he got from them surprised him. One of the consultants commented on the positive things that he saw but then challenged the principal. The consultant asked the principal to go back into that same classroom in the coming days, pick one student, and just sit with them— to witness a day in the life of one student and reflect on it.

So the principal went back into the classroom a day or two later and sat down with one student. He made it through an entire block with the student and noticed one concerning thing: The student he sat with did not interact with another human the entire time!

Learning Is Social

We know learning is social. It is not enough just to be on task, even if learning is going on. Yes, independent work has its place. However, it can be easy to create too much isolation between students, especially in a blended environment. We do not want to sacrifice human interaction for the sake of individualized online instruction. Compliance and quiet, on-task students should not be our primary metrics for success. Pay considerable attention to how students get opportunities to engage with others in meaningful ways during their stations (or any other blended model you choose to employ). Remember, collaboration can happen online or offline.

Chapter 3 Key Points

In this section, the important takeaways from the chapter are paired with the ISTE Standards for Educators that inform them.

- In the Station Rotation Model, students move through stations in teacher-developed groups for set periods of time. One of those stations should be small group instruction, and one of the stations should include some form of online learning. (Educator 5c, 6b)

- One of the first steps when planning for station rotation is to determine the number of groups, the number of stations, and how long groups will spend at each station. (Educator 6b)

- You do not have to stick with the textbook definition of the Station Rotation Model. Feel free to make adjustments based on the needs of your students. (Educator 5a, 5c)

- Be aware of the collaborative experiences you give students when they are not working directly with the teacher. Stations or any other blended activities should not be done completely independent of others. (Educator 3a, 5b)

- You are welcome to use the templates and resources in this chapter to plan your own station rotation lesson. (Educator 5a, 5b, 6a, 6b)

Reflection

After reading Chapter 3, take some time to consider how its ideas apply within your context using the questions below.

- Write or sketch your ideas for a station rotation that might work with your students. How many groups will you create? What kinds of stations would you use? How long would students stay at each station?

- What variations would you make to the traditional Station Rotation Model in your classroom? Why?

- What are the benefits of this model? What are the drawbacks?

Share your reflections and thoughts online using the hashtag #PerfectBlendBook.

CHAPTER 4

Implementing Personalized Learning in Your Blended Classroom

By the end of this chapter, you will:

- Review the differences between personalization and differentiation

- Explore the Flex Model and iterations of it, considering the use of playlists, choice boards, and checklists as tools to accomplish blended learning

- Consider how a hybrid approach between the Station Rotation and Flex Models might work best in some classrooms

ISTE Standards

This chapter addresses several ISTE Standards for Educators.

5. Designer

   Educators design authentic, learner-driven activities and environments that recognize and accommodate learner variability. Educators:

   a. Use technology to create, adapt and personalize learning experiences that foster independent learning and accommodate learner differences and needs.

   b. Design authentic learning activities that align with content area standards and use digital tools and resources to maximize active, deep learning.

   c. Explore and apply instructional design principles to create innovative digital learning environments that engage and support learning.

6. Facilitator

   Educators facilitate learning with technology to support student achievement of the 2016 ISTE Standards for Students. Educators:

   a. Foster a culture where students take ownership of their learning goals and outcomes in both independent and group settings.

   b. Manage the use of technology and student learning strategies in digital platforms, virtual environments, hands-on makerspaces or in the field.

7. Analyst

   Educators understand and use data to drive their instruction and support students in achieving their learning goals. Educators:

   a. Provide alternative ways for students to demonstrate competency and reflect on their learning using technology.

   b. Use technology to design and implement a variety of formative and summative assessments that accommodate learner needs, provide timely feedback to students and inform instruction.

Blended Learning as a Structure for Personalization

The terms *personalized learning* and *blended learning* often get thrown around like they are one and the same, frequently by software companies trying to promote personalization. However, blended learning is only a structure in which personalization can occur.

The Station Rotation Model for blended learning, for example, is great for differentiation, in which the teacher creates opportunities to individualize instruction to meet each student's needs, but it is not a naturally personalized model. With the Station Rotation Model, students do not own much of the learning. If you want to give students some autonomy over their learning, consider trying the Flex Model of blended learning.

The Flex Model of blended learning is similar to the Station Rotation Model in that students work on different activities, one of which is online learning, but it is driven by student-centered decisions. Students no longer move from one activity to another on a timed schedule and in fixed groups determined by the teacher. In the Flex Model, students have some choice in the learning activities, either over order, pace, activities, or all three. Many teachers who use a flex structure also incorporate flexible seating, allowing students to not only choose which activities they are completing or what their learning looks like during a particular time period, but also where that learning happens within the classroom.

If that all sounds like a classroom descending into chaos, don't be alarmed—it's not. The Flex Model still includes structure from the teacher. Personalizing instruction and giving students voice and choice does not mean students make *every* choice or that teachers no longer have a voice. It means students have some say over their learning in ways that make sense for your curriculum, classroom, students, and teaching style.

Tools to Implement the Flex Model

To personalize a blended lesson, teachers often use checklists, choice boards, playlists, and the like. Such tools allow you to create opportunities for student autonomy in different ways, depending on the goals for your classroom. As you reflect on these varied strategies for implementing the Flex Model, consider in what ways you want to honor student voice and choice. Is it in the timing and pacing of learning? Is it in the content? Is it a little of both? Each of these tools personalizes a different aspect of the blended classroom.

Before you get excited about a specific template or document, take some time to reflect. For your particular content area and group of students, what would you like the role of the student to be? What should they have control over? Where do your students need the most structure? Consider your thoughts on those questions as you explore checklists, choice boards, and playlists more deeply in the sections that follow.

Checklists

Of the Flex Model tools, checklists give teachers the most control over content. A *checklist* is a list of activities for the student to complete. The teacher controls at least some of the activities in the checklist. Students are told which tasks to complete, but the order and amount of time they take on each one is up to them. Checklists can be differentiated by creating different lists for different students.

A teacher can incorporate choice over content into a checklist by creating a section of Must Do (required) activities and a section of Can Do (optional) activities. If you include a section in the checklist of optional, student-selected activities, these Can Do tasks are generally completed after the mandatory activities are done.

If you choose to include Can Do activities in your checklist, I encourage you to make these activities as high-interest as possible. If the additional activities feel like undesirable work, what is the motivation for students to do anything beyond the minimum requirement? If these activities are something the students look forward to and are working toward, it can help keep them focused and engaged on the Must Do activities throughout the day or week as well.

Daily Checklists

DAILY CHECKLIST TEMPLATE

One option for checklists is to keep them simple and include tasks for just one lesson. A new checklist could be issued to students each day or with each lesson. You could provide these checklists on paper or in digital form. (For small checklists that you print, consider half sheets to save paper.) To help you get started, Figure 4.1 provides a template you can remix to use with your students. Get your own copy at **bit.ly /PBdailycheck** or by scanning the QR code.

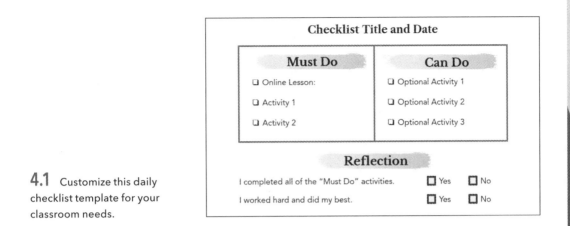

4.1 Customize this daily checklist template for your classroom needs.

Weekly Checklists

A common approach to using checklists is to create weekly checklists. As with daily checklists, you can include required (Must Do) items and optional (Can Do) activities. Plus, with weekly checklists, you can also identify activities that need to be completed daily and activities that need to be completed at some point during the week. The activities you include on these printed or digital checklists can be whatever fits your lesson plan. For them to be considered part of a blended learning environment, however, at least one of the activities must be an online learning activity.

Similar to when planning a station rotation in your classroom, try to mix up the activities so the blended learning time is both online and offline. Consider which activities are collaborative and which are independent, regardless of whether they are online or offline activities. You might even consider using the Station Rotation Planning Tool from Chapter 3 to plan out the activities on the checklist before creating the document that you give to students.

WEEKLY CHECKLIST TEMPLATE

If you would like some inspiration for your checklist, Figure 4.2 offers a template that you are free to remix and use with your students. Get your own copy at **bit.ly/PBweeklycheck**, or scan the QR code.

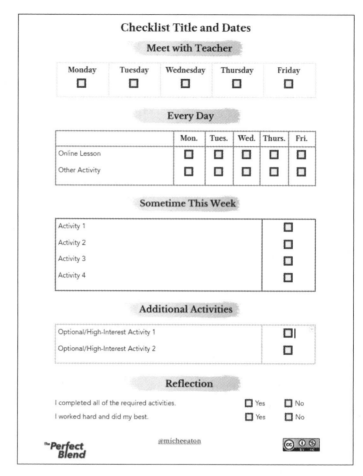

4.2 With this weekly checklist template, you can include activities students must complete daily, as well as activities that they must complete before the week's end.

Other Checklist Templates to Check Out

If you are looking for additional inspiration for your checklists, here are some other great options that you can find online:

Shuffle Checklist. Darcy Mueller created the music-themed checklist shown in Figure 4.3. Making your checklist look like a music streaming app highlights the idea that students can shuffle through activities in whatever order they would like (**bit.ly/musicappchecklist**).

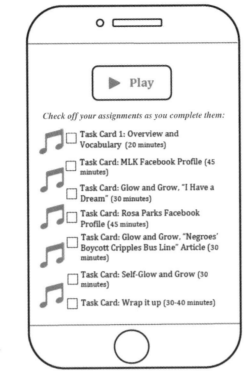

4.3 Darcy Mueller's Shuffle Checklist uses a music app theme to encourage students to work in whatever order they would like.

Simple Checklist. A checklist does not have to be fancy or picture-perfect. Something as simple as a Google Docs document can be used to quickly get up and running with checklists. Cisco Junior High School in Cisco, Texas, uses a checklist that's a great example of a simple approach to blended learning (**bit.ly/ciscocheck1**).

Calendar Checklist. Marcia Kish at DSD Professional Development offers another take on the use of Must Do and Can Do activities with her calendar-based, week-long checklist, found at **bit.ly/dsdcheck1**.

Playlists

A playlist is like a checklist taken up a notch. Like a full lesson, a good playlist incorporates student choice throughout and is more than a static list of activities for all students to complete. *Playlists* involve a combination of whole group learning, face-to-face opportunities,

**DOK PLAYLIST
TEMPLATE**

**DOK PLAYLIST
EXAMPLE**

and online learning, as well as individual, collaborative, and even small group learning. Playlists are very similar to *HyperDocs*, which are digital documents "where all components of a learning cycle have been pulled together into one central hub. Within a single document, students are provided with hyperlinks to all of the resources they need to complete that learning cycle" (Gonzalez, 2017).

One of my favorite examples of a high-quality playlist was designed by Steve Morris (@merc_morris). His playlist is based on different levels of depth of knowledge (DOK), and students must accumulate a certain number of points as they complete the playlist (**bit.ly/steveplaylist2**). They do not need to complete every task, but to get full points, they do need to complete activities from the higher DOK levels. He also created a handy template for this type of playlist in Google Docs (Figure 4.4, **bit.ly/steveplaylist1**).

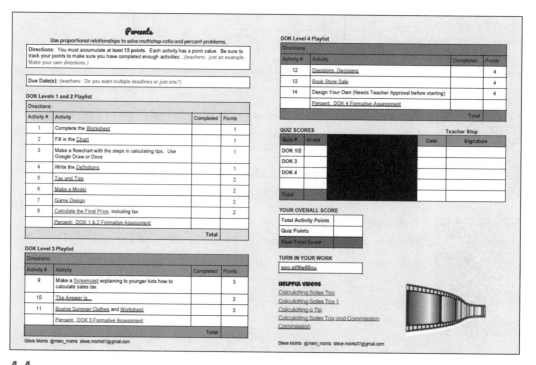

4.4 Use Steve Morris's playlist template to ensure students are completing activities at multiple DOK levels.

Here are some other playlist templates to check out:

 **Table Playlist.** This playlist comes from Cisco Junior High and is an example of how you can use a table in a Microsoft Word or Google Docs document to create a simple playlist for your students (**bit.ly/ciscoplaylist**).

 **Secondary School Playlists.** Steve Morris from Riverside USD in Riverside, California, developed a website with a list of several middle school and high school playlists. You can check out his extensive list of examples at **bit.ly/MSHSplaylists**.

 **Digital Menu.** Tom Spall (@tommyspall) designed a playlist like a restaurant menu using Google Slides. From this menu, students select an "appetizer," "entree," "beverage," and so on (Figure 4.5). Choice is a key component of this playlist. You can use the template at **bit.ly/learningmenu** to make your own version. Tom has other great digital menus worth checking out at **bit.ly/SpallMenus**.

MENU PLAYLIST TEMPLATE

SPALL DIGITAL MENUS

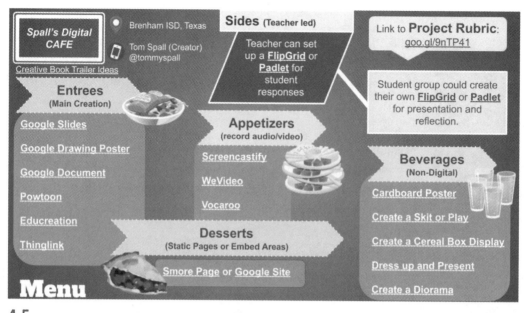

4.5 Tom Spall's restaurant menu is a clever way to create a playlist that encourages student choice.

Choice Boards

Choice boards generally incorporate the most student choice. Activities are organized in a grid, often like a tic-tac-toe board or bingo board. Students make choices about what activities they do and mark them on the choice board as they finish. Teachers can choose to set specific stipulations as well. For instance, you could have students do activities to complete a straight line like in tic-tac-toe. Students could be told to select whatever activities they want from the board, but you set a minimum number to be completed. Most standard choice boards are three-by-three grids, but you can include as many activities as you would like, depending on the complexity of each activity and the amount of time you plan to use one choice board.

Choice boards have been around for a while and are a great example of how you can leverage some of the strategies you are already doing well to create a successful blended learning experience for your students. Remember, for it to be considered blended learning, at least one component of the choice board should include online learning of some kind. You might consider making the middle square in the choice board the starting point for students. Put a digital lesson there that everyone completes. Then have them choose the rest of the activities that they would like to do from around the board.

**CHOICE BOARD
TEMPLATE**

Activities can be hands-on and available outside of the choice board. You could organize the activities in folders or bins around the room to encourage students to get up and move. Each activity's instructions or materials could also be linked inside a digital choice board.

You can use the simple choice board template in Figure 4.6 as a starting point and make adjustments based on the needs of your classroom. Get your editable version at **bit.ly/PBchoice** or scan the QR code.

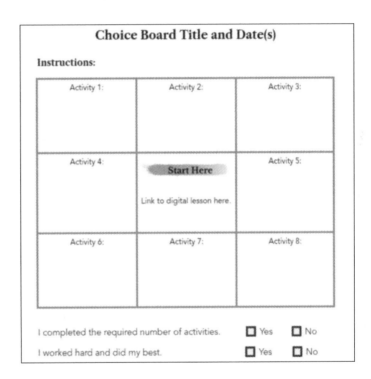

4.6 This simple choice board template can be customized to your students' needs.

If you would like to explore some updated versions of the choice board, the following resources show how you can put a new spin on the standard choice board:

Four Cs Choice Board. Marcia Kish from DSD Professional Development (@dsdpd) designed a Four Cs Choice Board on which each of the activities is aligned to at least one of the Four Cs (communication, collaboration, creativity, and critical thinking). From her website (**bit.ly/dsdchoice**), you can download the choice board template, as well as corresponding direction cards for each of the activities on the choice board.

Tic-Tac-Toe Choice Menu. Kasey Bell of Shake Up Learning (@shakeuplearning) created a simple, but brilliant, choice board (**bit.ly/shakeupchoice**) that puts a new spin on the tic-tac-toe board and offers students structured choice. Students complete the board's middle activity first, then select a blue square and a yellow square to complete three in a row. This color-coded approach allows you to be strategic in placing activities on the board. You could cover one skill but make all the blue activities independent and all the yellow activities collaborative. You could make one set of activities online and the other set offline. You could even cover two different skills or topics in this way. When I have used this template, I made the middle square the online lesson. This particular template gives students structured choice.

DOK Choice Board. The tic-tac-toe-style board designed by Education Elements uses depth of knowledge (DOK) as a way to organize each activity (**bit.ly/eechoicel**). If you use this template and create activities that align with the various levels of DOK, students will end up doing a variety of activities at different depths of knowledge. The middle square is required of all students and is the highest DOK activity. This template also features a place to put a link to Google Forms to collect completed choice boards. This is one option for students to submit their work. You may also have students physically turn in their choice board.

Hybrid Approach to the Flex Model

Keep in mind that you do not have to stick to one concrete model of blended learning. Your perfect blend should not be an exact replica of another classroom, following a rigid recipe. As you play around with these models in your classroom, you may find that a hybrid approach makes the most sense.

You could switch between stations and using one of the flex tools from this chapter based on the lesson or content you are teaching. You could also find a combination of the two models that makes sense for your classroom.

You could merge more personalization into your stations by making the options you give students be physical stations that they go to. Students could self-select stations and spend a set period of time at each one.

Another option is to consider scheduling different formats for specific days. For example, here is a sample schedule that combines direct instruction, station rotation, and the Flex Model.

- Monday: Whole group direct instruction
- Tuesday: Station rotation with small group instruction
- Wednesday: Station rotation with small group instruction
- Thursday: Flex Model (checklist, choice board, or playlist) with individual conferences
- Friday: Flex Model (checklist, choice board, or playlist) with individual conferences

Another option is to create checklists for students in which one of the activities is a choice board. This gives you control over the Must Do activities, while building in some student autonomy opportunities.

Basically, the options are endless. Start somewhere, and then continue to evolve and tweak the model so that it fits the individual needs of your students. Remember, *you* are the architect of your classroom experience, and that experience should be very personal and unique to your specific classroom.

Chapter 4 Key Points

In this section, the important takeaways from the chapter are paired with the ISTE Standards for Educators that inform them.

- The Flex Model of blended learning is a great option to include more student voice and choice into the classroom. (Educator 5a, 5b, 6a)
- In the Flex Model, students have some choice in the learning activities, either over order, pace, activities, or all three. (Educator 5a, 5b, 6a)
- When using checklists, students complete activities selected by the teacher. At least some of them are Must Do activities. Students have control over the pace and order in which they complete these activities. (Educator 5a, 5b, 5c, 6b, 7b)

- Playlists are like full lessons. They involve a combination of whole group learning, face-to-face opportunities, and online learning, as well as individual, collaborative, and even small group learning. (Educator 5a, 5b, 5c, 6b, 7b)

- Choice boards have activities that are organized in a grid, similar to a tic-tac-toe board or bingo board. (Educator 5a, 5b, 5c, 6b, 7a, 7b)

- Any of the tools or models discussed in this chapter could be altered or combined to create a unique experience for your students. (Educator 5a, 5c, 6b, 7b)

Reflection

After reading Chapter 4, take some time to consider how its ideas apply within your context using the questions below.

- Which of the tools discussed in this chapter are you most interested in exploring for your own classroom?

- What adjustments would you make to these tools or blended learning structures to fit the needs of your individual classroom?

- What are the benefits of the Flex Model? What are the drawbacks?

- Think about an upcoming lesson or unit. What aspects will require teacher differentiation? Where are the opportunities for personalization for students?

Share your reflections and thoughts online using the hashtag #PerfectBlendBook.

CHAPTER 5

Classroom Management in a Modern Learning Environment

By the end of this chapter, you will:

- Understand the guidelines and expectations that need to be in place for a blended learning environment to run smoothly

- Gain ideas for transitioning students from one station to the next

- Learn ways to provide technical support while meeting with small groups

- Understand how to align your classroom layout with the instructional outcomes you hope to achieve

ISTE Standards

This chapter addresses several ISTE Standards for Educators.

3. Citizen

   Educators inspire students to positively contribute to and responsibly participate in the digital world. Educators:

   c. Mentor students in safe, legal and ethical practices with digital tools and the protection of intellectual rights and property.

4. Collaborator

   Educators dedicate time to collaborate with both colleagues and students to improve practice, discover and share resources and ideas, and solve problems. Educators:

   b. Collaborate and co-learn with students to discover and use new digital resources and diagnose and troubleshoot technology issues.

6. Facilitator

   Educators facilitate learning with technology to support student achievement of the 2016 ISTE Standards for Students. Educators:

   b. Manage the use of technology and student learning strategies in digital platforms, virtual environments, hands-on makerspaces or in the field.

Classroom Management in a Blended Learning Environment

Now that you are beginning to formulate ideas for the structures you might try within your classroom, we need to address the details that help make a blended classroom run smoothly. A classroom where students have a voice and are not necessarily doing everything their neighbor is doing can feel like organized chaos. Don't worry: You can manage this type of environment and provide structure while still honoring the unique voices and needs of the students in your classroom. The solution lies in a combination of classroom management protocols and procedures, along with how you organize the physical classroom environment (more on this aspect later).

A major part of creating a classroom culture that is conducive to blended learning is establishing clear guidelines and expectations with your students. Teaching students how to take ownership of their learning is no small task, and providing appropriate structure is the key to success. When giving flexibility to students, communicate the importance of mutual respect for each person in the classroom, as students will move from working independently to collaborating frequently. Additionally, as students work in online spaces, it becomes even more critical that we regularly engage students in learning what it means to be a good digital citizen. Students must learn how to appropriately interact with others online while keeping themselves safe.

Device Management

Establishing and practicing routines for storage, distribution, and movement with devices will help each blended lesson run smoothly. Do not assume that students inherently know how to do these things. As you introduce technology into the blended classroom, be clear about the rules regarding where students can work with the devices and when and where devices can be left unattended. Specific protocols help maintain a structured environment. In addition, the more organized and explicit you are with instructions for how to care for the technology in the room, the more likely you are to avoid unnecessary breaks and damages that impede your ability to facilitate blended learning.

It is also important for students to remember that it may not be appropriate to be on technology at all times. When you need to address the entire class, have a protocol in place to quickly switch students' attention from their devices to you. I recommend the phrase *put your screens at 45*. Teach students that if you say this, all laptop or Chromebook screens need to be lowered to a 45° angle. This helps students focus on you without logging them out of their devices. If you are in a classroom that uses tablets, the same thing can be accomplished by flipping the device upside down.

Transitions for Stations

If you are an elementary teacher, you probably have lots of ideas for effective ways to transition students from one station to another, even if you have never implemented blended learning in your classroom. When you introduce a lot of movement into your classroom, as you would see in a Station Rotation Model, for example, it is important to be able to get students' attention and help them quickly and effectively transition from one space to another. This is important regardless of the age of the students.

"1, 2, 3"

One strategy that might be successful in your room is to establish expectations one step at a time for students. For example, you could teach your students that when you methodically announce "1, 2, 3," they should complete a certain task at each number. On 1, for instance, they should finish up what they are working on. On 2, they should clean up their spaces and prepare to transition. Then on 3, they should push in their chairs and quietly move to the next station.

I have seen this done without interrupting the teacher by timing each phase of the rotation using Microsoft PowerPoint. You can put information for each station on a slide, and then set each slide to automatically play for an allotted amount of time. You could set up slides for the 1, 2, or 3 signals and have them run automatically without having to stop or interrupt your small group.

Timers

Simple timers are great tools, and you can find plenty of options online. For a quick solution, a Google search for "timer" provides an actual timer you can click to set and activate, as well as links to more choices in the search results. Visible timers are helpful because they show students how much time is left for each station, which, in turn, can help keep students on task. If students know there is a finite amount of time to get a task done, they are more likely to stay focused and get it done. It also can be helpful just to know that an activity does have an end to keep students motivated and engaged.

When you use timers of any kind, however, keep an eye on the stress levels of the room. You want to avoid using timers if their countdown effect causes your students to panic. We do not want to put unnecessary pressure on our students because we are now timing every activity. Sometimes a visible timer may not be appropriate. That will be based on the nature of the activity and the students in your room.

Sounds and Music

Instead of raising your voice to be heard over a group of students engaged in learning, using sounds and music can be an effective way to keep things running smoothly in your blended classroom. For instance, you can use simple sounds, such as a bell or an alarm on your

ClassroomScreen

ClassroomScreen (**classroomscreen.com**) is a favorite classroom management tool among teachers I work with. This tool gives you a customizable dashboard with tools to help you manage independent work, including:

- Random name picker
- Sound level monitor
- Text box for instructions
- Traffic light for visual transitions or indicators
- Timer

CLASSROOM-SCREEN DEMO

If you have multiple groups working concurrently in your classroom, you can even divide the screen and set up separate tools, such as timers, for each group. You then project your customized ClassroomScreen dashboard to the board so all students can see it. For a quick demonstration of ClassroomScreen, check out the video at **bit.ly/ClassScreen** or scan the QR code.

phone, to indicate to students they need to clean up and prepare themselves to transition to another activity. I have even heard of teachers purchasing inexpensive doorbells with multiple sounds as a novel way to help students manage time.

Another nondisruptive strategy could be to use music. You could teach your students that once the music comes on, they have until the end of the song to finish up what they are working on, clean up, and move to the next station. I like this strategy because it does not stop the teacher's work with the small group and helps students learn to manage their time independently.

Share Your Transitions

TRANSITION IDEAS

If you have ideas for transitions that work well in your classroom, share them with other readers (and find a few more) by visiting the Padlet wall at **padlet.com/michele_eaton/transition**.

Technology Support Strategies

If your students are using technology or working independently in any capacity while you provide small group instruction, you need to have a way for them to get help when you are not readily available to stop and assist. You probably know this problem all too well. Sometimes it seems like students will have no questions for you until the moment you are unavailable. This will only be magnified when you begin to introduce digital lessons into the mix. Several strategies will help you manage this phenomenon.

Student Experts

When I was in the classroom, the students in my class were all assigned jobs. Students that were exceptionally techy-savvy, I gave the job of providing technology support in the classroom. Any time we were working on a blended lesson online and I was unavailable, students that ran into a problem knew to go to our technology support team first.

This was successful in that we found a way to have the students utilize the expertise in the room while I was unavailable, but it created a couple of problems, too. The biggest problem was that the work of the same two or three students was constantly disrupted so they could assist their peers in troubleshooting. At the same time, the other students were not building capacity to solve problems or troubleshoot issues.

Kristin Ziemke, co-author of the book *Amplify*, visited my school district recently and led a technology-infused lesson in one of our primary classrooms. Without knowing our students personally or being able to quickly spot the tech-savvy kids, she successfully helped students identify themselves as experts to help their classmates. Instead of selecting a specific set of students to be the technology support from the beginning, she found experts as the lesson progressed. When she had to stop and help a student troubleshoot something, she would end their interaction by announcing to the class that if anyone else experienced that particular issue, this student was now the expert and could help.

I appreciated this approach to student experts for two reasons. One, the same students were not shouldering the burden of solving all of their friends' technology issues; that job was instead shared among all the students. Two, it emphasized a growth mindset. Instead of selecting students to be experts who were predisposed to be good with technology, she helped students see their growth from struggling with something to becoming an expert. What an incredible message to send to our students!

Collaborative Support Documents

Another strategy that gets all your students helping each other is to use an online collaborative document with the whole class. I saw this strategy first used in Amanda Moore's (@teachforthewin) fourth-grade blended classroom. She created a simple Google document with a table that she shared with all of her students. It had columns for the student's name, their question, and a response to the question. The document was then projected onto the screen. The original instructions were for the students to add to the table when they had a question. Amanda planned to respond to the students' questions when she had a free moment between small groups.

What was incredible was how this protocol evolved on its own. Instead of waiting for their teacher to respond to the questions, students naturally went in and typed responses to the questions. When Amanda checked the table, she was pleasantly surprised to see that her students had quietly taken care of each other's questions and she had very little she needed to respond to (Figure 5.1). I love this strategy for encouraging community without disrupting the learning going on in the classroom.

Name	Question	Responses
Adriana	I can't get the video to play.	I will come help you! Manuel
Jordan W.	Can someone help me with the practice? I keep getting the wrong answers.	Your group is next. Go back to the video and watch it. Then I can help you in a second. -Mrs. Moore
Erik	How do you change the color of your words?	Do you see the letter A in the toolbar? Click it. If you don't see it, I can show you. -Adriana

5.1 An example of Amanda's collaborative document for technology support

Share Your Strategies

TECH SUPPORT IDEAS

What strategies work for you to help answer students' questions when you are working with a small group? Share your ideas and see what other readers have to say by visiting the Padlet wall at **padlet.com /michele_eaton/techsupport**.

Designing the Physical Classroom to Successfully Implement Blended Learning

How you design the physical space of your classroom can greatly impact the success of your blended learning implementation. The classroom environment must align with the learning outcomes you have planned. With increased student agency, a more flexible learning space becomes necessary.

Form Follows Function

If you want students to work collaboratively, have a voice in the learning activities they engage with, and move efficiently from one activity to the next, a traditional classroom setup could make that instructional shift unnecessarily difficult. This also does not mean you need an architect, a budget for expensive furniture, and a layout that makes your classroom feel like a coffee shop. It simply means if you want to encourage student agency and personalization, then you need to have spaces in your classroom that honor student choice and the movement that comes along with many blended learning strategies.

I think it is easy to get lost in picking out flexible furniture because it is trendy or makes the space look modern. When we design our physical environment, form should follow function. Movable furniture is great, for instance, if we need students actively moving and setting up new spaces to meet the goals of the learning. If your blended classroom strategy will rely heavily on differentiation set up by the teacher, where the students move from one space to another on a set schedule, simply grouping students to create collaborative workspaces could be sufficient.

If you want to create more flexibility for students, give them options and choices about where they work in the classroom. Consider creating spaces for quiet independent work and also spaces for collaboration with the ability for students to move freely into those spaces. As you design these zones in the classroom that students can move in and out of, think about the different functions of learning you need each space to accommodate. Do you have spaces for:

- Quiet independent work
- Small group collaboration
- Demonstration
- Making and creating
- Organizing materials and supplies

Redesign Resources

If you are looking for a great resource on redesigning learning spaces, I highly recommend the book *The Space: A Guide for Educators* by Rebecca Hare and Dr. Robert Dillon. The book has several ideas for how you can design spaces that support learning.

5.2 *The Space: A Guide for Educators* by Rebecca Louise Hare and Dr. Robert Dillon

As you rethink the structure of the learning in your classroom, the need for a large direct instruction space may diminish. In an article for *EdTech Magazine* (2017), Eric Patnoudes (@NoApp4Pedagogy) encouraged teachers to consider the amount of space the teacher's desk and space in the front of the room take up that could be used for more flexible learning. As you redesign your classroom, try to remove the idea of the "front of the room" or even the space dedicated to your filing cabinets, and focus on creating multiple work zones around the room that serve various instructional purposes.

Patnoudes also suggested that this design work does not have to happen on your own and that students can be given input on this design as well (2017). You might be surprised at how inventive students can be if they have a say in the structure of their room. Dr. Robert Dillon, co-author of the book *The Space: A Guide for Educators* (2016), suggests explicitly asking your students what in the room is supporting their learning and what is getting in the way of it. If we truly want to encourage student voice and choice, then that should be reflected even in the design choices we make in our physical learning spaces.

Redesign on a Budget

Although some of you may be lucky enough to be in a building outfitted with the latest and greatest in active learning furniture solutions, the reality is that the furniture you have available to you is largely out of your control. However, you easily can make budget-friendly changes to your classroom environment that encourage a more collaborative, flexible, student-driven learning experience.

My first suggestion is to ask. I always like to say, "don't ask; don't get." If you want to remove individual desks in exchange for more collaborative workspaces, talk to your principal. See if the principal knows of any tables available in the building or in surplus in the district. Brainstorm with the leadership in your building to come up with creative solutions. Come prepared to the conversation with a focus on the learning outcomes and experiences you want to create and how the right furniture could play a role in that. The worst they can say is that they do not have access to anything, which does not leave you any worse off than when you started. The best outcome is that there are resources available and waiting that you did not know about.

You could also look for pre-owned furniture or ask the parents of your students if they have anything they would want to donate to the classroom. Be careful when doing this, though. Know what you are allowed to bring in from outside before you ask. Often, schools will have rules about bringing in furniture with any kind of fabric, for example. You do not want to inadvertently introduce critters or allergens into your classroom.

Personally, I like to shop sales. You can find beanbags, crates, cushions, and more on sale, especially when they are out of season. I can always find great deals after the back-to-college rush. If you are near a university, you might ask around about any sales that graduating seniors often organize near the end of the school year. Crowd-sourcing websites (such as

DonorsChoose.org or **GoFundMe.com**), fundraisers, and grants are other sources of funding that can help you redesign your learning space without breaking the bank.

Different types of seating can be great. You do not need new furniture, though. Rearranging your existing furniture can go a long way toward a more personalized, flexible space. Group desks together in different arrangements, from independent stations to small groups to arrangements that encourage discussion.

Think about inexpensive ways that you can make the furniture in your room easy to move. If you do not have access to furniture on wheels, make your current furniture more mobile. With permission, you could add chair casters to the bottom of the furniture or use furniture glides to help make moving chairs and tables easier and quicker.

**CLASSROOM
DESIGN IDEAS**

Teachers are often experts at finding ways to "hack" their classroom space. What creative solutions do you use to organize your classroom and create flexible learning spaces for students on a budget? Share your ideas with the readers by visiting the Padlet wall at **padlet.com/michele_eaton/redesign**.

Know that, just like many transformations, redesigning your classroom will likely be a process. Tinker and update as you can, ensuring that you are getting student feedback along the way. Ultimately, we should not be designing our classrooms to impress other teachers on Pinterest or Instagram. We should be designing these spaces to improve learning for our students.

Chapter 5 Key Points

In this section, the important takeaways from the chapter are paired with the ISTE Standards for Educators that inform them.

- Even though blended learning environments should encourage student autonomy and agency, structure and classroom management are imperative for success. (Educator 6b)

- As students work in online spaces, it becomes even more critical that you regularly engage students in learning to be good digital citizens. (Educator 3c)

- Set up protocols for device management, transitioning between activities, and how to provide support to students when they are busy working with small groups. (Educator 4b, 6b)

- Align your physical classroom layout with the instructional goals of your blended classroom. (Educator 6b)

- Student voice is not only important when it comes to instruction and assessment. In addition, you should regularly get feedback and ideas from your students about how to organize the classroom environment to enhance their learning. (Educator 4b)

Reflection

After reading Chapter 5, take some time to consider how its ideas apply within your context using the questions below.

- What classroom management strategies stood out to you that you want to implement?

- Are there other aspects of a blended classroom that require protocols and guidelines that are not mentioned in this chapter?

- What is getting in the way of personalized learning in your classroom space?

- What would your dream classroom look like if you had endless funds to design the ideal learning experience? Grab a scrap of paper or an online drawing tool and sketch it out.

- Now, consider your current classroom: What hacks or adjustments could you make on a very limited budget to move your space toward that ideal learning environment you just sketched out? How does it help facilitate the blended learning model you designed?

Share your reflections and thoughts online using the hashtag #PerfectBlendBook.

PART 2

The Digital Classroom

CHAPTER 6

Reading Print vs. Reading Digital Content

By the end of this chapter, you will:

- Be familiar with the research surrounding how we read online

- Understand the difference between learning and reading online and learning and reading in a traditional environment

- Understand the importance of designing digital content with these learning differences in mind

- Understand the importance of introducing varied text types, both print and digital, to students

- Learn strategies for designing digital text for the way we read online

- Learn active reading strategies to encourage students to engage deeply with digital text

- Reflect on what content you should put online and what content you should deliver in a more traditional way

ISTE Standards

This chapter addresses several ISTE Standards for Educators.

1. Learner

   Educators continually improve their practice by learning from and with others and exploring proven and promising practices that leverage technology to improve student learning. Educators:

   a. Set professional learning goals to explore and apply pedagogical approaches made possible by technology and reflect on their effectiveness.

   c. Stay current with research that supports improved student learning outcomes, including findings from the learning sciences.

5. Designer

   Educators design authentic, learner-driven activities and environments that recognize and accommodate learner variability. Educators:

   b. Design authentic learning activities that align with content area standards and use digital tools and resources to maximize active, deep learning.

   c. Explore and apply instructional design principles to create innovative digital learning environments that engage and support learning.

7. Analyst

   Educators understand and use data to drive their instruction and support students in achieving their learning goals. Educators:

   b. Use technology to design and implement a variety of formative and summative assessments that accommodate learner needs, provide timely feedback to students and inform instruction.

Rethinking Instruction in a Digital Space

One of the biggest misconceptions about using online learning in any capacity has to do with what quality looks like. People often think that if they just move high-quality face-to-face instruction online, that they will end up with high-quality online learning. They won't.

As a matter of fact, I think this misguided approach to creating online instruction is the very reason so many people do not think online learning is as effective as more traditional instruction. As an advocate for online and blended education, I believe we can teach just about anything online and do it just as well as we can without technology. For that to happen, however, we have to design these online experiences differently. If all we ever try to do is replicate face-to-face instruction, then online learning will never be more than a cheap imitation of the traditional experience.

One key to designing effective online experiences is to understand that how we read digital text is much different than how we read print materials. The truth is, we don't read online—we skim. Research from as early as 1997 has found that we are programmed to scan and skim online text (Nielsen, 1997), while a 2014 study revealed 55% of us spend fewer than *fifteen seconds* actively viewing any given web page (Haile, 2014).

Just think about that for a second. When you grab a book to read, you are often committing to focused reading, to read that book word for word until you finish it. Contrast that to typical internet use: We do a quick Google search for a fact or figure, then hunt and skim for just that piece of information. We have essentially trained our brains that this is how to read on the internet. Yet, we often introduce a digital text to students in the same way that we would hand them a book. This needs to change. We must be more intentional about how we design digital text and the active reading strategies we employ to accompany digital text.

Comprehension of Digital Text

Because of our inclination to skim online text, several studies show that readers experience a small dip in comprehension when reading digitally versus in print. In addition to skimming, there are many other factors that contribute to a dip in comprehension when reading online.

For example, the spatial information we have when reading print helps us with comprehension as compared to digital text (Ross, Pechenkina, Aeschliman, & Chase, 2017). Imagine holding a piece of paper or a book. When you can physically see the text, it is easier to picture where you saw a piece of information. This helps students when looking back in a text to answer a question or refer back to some content in the reading. We do not have that spatial information as readily available to us when scrolling through an online article or ebook. It becomes harder to visualize where in the text you read a piece of information, which in turn makes it more difficult to remember. This is especially true when students need the text to answer questions or do an activity after reading.

Print reading is also much more linear than digital reading. When you read a book, you generally start at the beginning and move your way to the end. You can see and feel how much of the book you have left. Reading online is much different. With hyperlinks and the ability to chase any thought to a different site, reading online is much less linear. This stream of consciousness approach to reading makes it difficult to focus in on what you are reading, potentially having a negative impact on comprehension (Schwartz, 2016).

The same studies that show a loss in comprehension online also note that it is not because of the medium per se, but more attributed to distraction, which leads to shallow reading. These distractions come in the form of online design when changes in colors, screens, movement, and so on cause distraction (Konnikova, 2014). Interestingly, studies have found that online gamers work better with these distractions because they are used to staying focused with shifting media (Coiro, 2011).

In addition, the very nature of the internet creates distractions with endless numbers of resources to view, both on-topic and not. Julie Coiro from the University of Rhode Island found that it takes an increasing amount of attention to read online because of the seemingly unending number of choices and access to information we have online (Korbey, 2018). We are always one hyperlink away from additional information, both relevant and irrelevant. And that is without even mentioning the number of ways our attention can be diverted from reading due to notifications, social media, games, and other digital distractors.

Geoff Kaufman and Mary Flanagan (2016), researchers from Carnegie Mellon, did some specific research on this very subject. In an experiment on comprehension of digital text versus print text, Flanagan and Kaufman found that online reading led to a greater focus on concrete details but that print reading was superior for making inferences and identifying the gist of a text. For their experiment, they observed comprehension of both fiction and nonfiction text in a print format and in a digital PDF format. The PDF was viewed from a screen but had no identifiable distractors available, such as hyperlinks or other opportunities for interactivity. Readers were given a short story by David Sedaris to read and a table of car facts and specifications. A quiz was given after each reading. Those people who read the story and the table in a digital format scored higher than their print counterparts on recalling facts and details. However, those participants who read the materials in print scored higher on questions where they had to identify meaning or inferences in the short story and were also more likely to choose the best car to purchase from the table.

In similar but slightly conflicting research, Patricia Greenfield (Subrahmanyam, et al., 2013) from the University of California found that multitasking while reading online slowed readers down, but their basic comprehension remained unaffected as compared to those reading in print or reading online without multitasking. When the participants in the study were asked to synthesize multiple texts with multitasking or without multitasking either in print or online, the medium did not influence comprehension. However, when multitasking was present, participants were less likely to comprehend and synthesize at a higher level. One specific detail Greenfield's research found was that taking notes on paper while reading digital text significantly improved reading comprehension. It is also important to note that other research (Ben-Yehudah & Eshet-Alkalai, 2014) has found that digital reading platforms that incorporate annotation tools can also close that comprehension gap we see when reading online.

Closing the Comprehension Gap

If comprehension suffers when reading online, shouldn't we just stick with print text? Why is there such a trend toward digital materials?

I would like you to pause and reflect on your own personal and professional reading in the past week. Grab a piece of paper or make a quick note on your computer. Try to list all of the things you have read in the past week, from books and blog posts to emails and text messages to social media posts and magazines.

What do you notice? Most likely you interacted with a wide variety of text just in the past seven days. There are clear challenges with digital media and online text, but it's not going anywhere. As you can probably tell from your own reflection, the amount of digital text we are exposed to is growing every year. As a matter of fact, 2011 marked the first year that Amazon sold more ebooks than paper books (Miller & Bosman, 2011).

To truly prepare students for modern reading, ignoring digital text would be doing them a disservice. In her book *Reader, Come Home: The Reading Brain in a Digital World*, Maryanne Wolf (2019) discussed the importance of helping students develop biliterate reading brains. With a biliterate brain, a student can essentially "code-switch" between both print and digital text, being literate in both.

We know from the research shared in this chapter that we cannot approach both forms of reading in the exact same way, though. We must actively and intentionally design digital reading experiences to help our students learn the skills they need to comprehend digital text in deep, meaningful ways and close that comprehension gap between print and online mediums. We can do this by building on the strengths of digital media while addressing its limitations head on.

Designing Scannable Text

We can address what we know about how we read online in two ways. We can design text knowing that our students are likely to skim it, or we can design reading activities that encourage deeper reading. It is helpful to be skilled in both of these areas. How you approach reading in your digital content depends on the objective for any particular lesson or activity.

If the goal of the text is not sustained reading and you just want the students to efficiently take in material, it can be helpful to know how to redesign text to ensure maximum comprehension. One way you can do this is by making the text *scannable*.

Keywords

To draw your reader's attention to important points while scanning a text, you need to be able to draw attention to keywords quickly and easily. One way to do this is by highlighting important vocabulary. Chapter 7 offers detailed suggestions on this, as well as cautions regarding color selections and the amount of color you use. When you follow a few guidelines, however, highlighting keywords can be a helpful and effective way to draw students' attention to important content.

As people read online, we know that they often read the first few words of a line or sentence and then move on to the next. This is commonly how readers scan digital text. Knowing this, you can strategically write text by front-loading keywords at the beginning of sentences. Even if your students scan the text and miss the ends of the sentences, they will read the most important vocabulary.

Headings and Lists

Often when scanning a digital text, readers will use headings and subheadings to quickly move their eyes down the screen. Using frequent and informative headings throughout the text can help the reader get the gist of the writing. Keep in mind, subheadings that are descriptive and adequately summarize the section are better than focusing on clever or abstract titles.

Bulleted lists are another digital writing strategy to help ensure readers are maximizing their comprehension. Bulleted lists are easy to scan and quickly read. Consider the digital text you write in your lessons. If there are paragraphs that could be turned into a list, making that adjustment might be beneficial.

Paragraph Organization

Just like users will likely skim and read the beginning of sentences or lines on the screen without finishing them, the same can be said for paragraphs. It is common for readers to read the beginning of a paragraph and skip to the next paragraph when they feel they have taken in the gist of the information. Knowing that your readers are likely to scan the text in this way, it can be helpful to include only one key point per paragraph.

If you write about more than one thing in a paragraph, readers who are scanning the text are likely to stop reading before getting to the second or third idea. By keeping each paragraph to a singular idea, readers will not miss the introduction of new content.

You might also consider organizing the paragraphs in your digital text according to importance, with the most important information at the beginning of the text. Many modern journalists use this *inverted pyramid* strategy when writing news stories (Figure 6.1). They start the article with the most newsworthy information or the main idea, follow it up with the important details, then end the piece with other general supporting information that is less critical to the article as a whole.

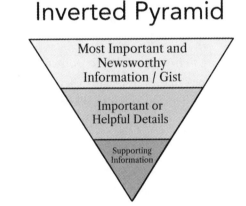

Inverted Pyramid

Most Important and Newsworthy Information / Gist

Important or Helpful Details

Supporting Information

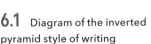

6.1 Diagram of the inverted pyramid style of writing

The thought behind the inverted pyramid style of writing is that it ensures equitable comprehension for all readers, regardless of how much of the article each person reads. A person who reads the whole text will read the most important information along with enriching supporting details. A person who reads only the beginning of the article will still walk away with the most important information.

Keep the Reading Purpose in Mind

As you are writing digital text or introducing digital text to students, view it through the lens of someone who would scan the writing. If the goal is content acquisition and not sustained, deep reading, finding or creating more easily scannable text might be a useful strategy. In subsequent chapters, we will do a deep dive into designing digital content to help our students process information efficiently and effectively. This information will also contribute to designing digital text and multimedia for the way that we naturally read online.

Active Reading Strategies

When the goal is to help students read text *deeply* online, simply designing scannable text is not enough. We want to help students learn how to actively read all types of text, whether print or digital. Fortunately, there are strategies you can try when delivering online text to students to help ensure comprehension and an equitable reading experience when compared to more traditional print reading. Let's take a look at some examples of deep reading strategies to help disrupt the pattern of skimming and scanning digital text.

In-Class Digital Reading

Any opportunity you can find to help students slow down and reflect on their digital reading will be helpful. This can be done strategically when students are reading synchronously during class, either as part of independent work or whole-group instruction.

First and foremost, it is critical that as a teacher, you are modeling multiple text resources to your students. For example, read-alouds should not just be picture books. In addition to print resources, introduce varied formats, such as ebooks, blogs, infographics, and so on. In *Taming the Wild Text*, Pam Allyn and Monica Burns (2017) recommend using anchor charts for digital texts. Much like elementary teachers create anchor charts for how to navigate nonfiction print text, consider creating anchor charts to discuss the differences readers see with various digital materials. How you read an infographic is very different from how you would read a printed magazine article on the same topic, for instance.

It is not necessary for you to have one device for every student to make active reading of digital text work, either. I prefer a 2:1 device setup for in-class digital reading and activities.

If two students are working at one device, you can create cooperative activities that can be really effective. Have one student be the "driver" and one student be the "navigator." The driver is the student responsible for touching the device. The navigator gives verbal instructions to the driver about what to click. Then have the students switch roles. If you are having students complete an activity of some kind with their reading or after viewing multimedia material, this type of activity can keep students focused, collaborating, and engaged in on-task behavior.

Devin Hess, Director of Educational Technology for the UC Berkeley History-Social Science Project, shared a four-step approach to deep reading of digital content that focuses on getting students to slow down and meaningfully engage with the reading. The four key elements to any active reading strategy, according to Hess are:

1. Slow down: Help students move through the text slowly and deliberately.

2. Active engagement: Have the students actively participate in the reading, either through reading response, annotation, note-taking, or other reading strategy.

3. Oral discourse: Move the students' attention away from the screen and to each other. Have students talk out loud and discuss the reading with their peers.

4. Reflection: Have the students reflect on their reading. (Schwartz, 2016)

Create a Road Map

Because of the lack of spatial information we have when reading online, navigating and comprehending digital text can be a challenge. Noted literacy consultant Kristina Smekens stated, "If students don't know where they are in the text while reading, they will have an even harder time going back and finding the information after reading" (2017). To combat this, Smekens recommends helping students create a road map of their reading by taking notes on paper. This does not have to be fancy. Simply give students scratch paper. While they read, have them jot down important details in a list on that paper. This helps students visualize and track their reading, like a road map for their digital text (2017).

Mixing paper-and-pencil activities with digital reading also helps combat the eye fatigue we can experience from looking at a screen for too long. It also means that students don't have to flip between multiple tabs to take notes or actively engage with the text. Sometimes the best tool to use for a job is not technology.

Using Collaborative Documents

Creating opportunities for annotation can be a great way to encourage active reading of digital text. Unfortunately, many teachers may not have access to online reading platforms with annotation tools built in. You can, however, improvise. If you have access to Google Drive, Microsoft OneDrive, or another collaborative document tool, you have a whole range of annotation tools at your fingertips for free.

By copying a digital text into a collaborative document (making sure to provide proper attribution and ensuring that you are not breaking copyright or fair use in the process), you enable students to use tools such as comments, highlights, or even writing in the document to mark up the text as they read.

Headings and Highlights

UC Berkeley's Devin Hess also recommends a reading strategy called "Headings and Highlights" (Schwartz, 2016). This strategy is simple:

1. Copy and paste a digital text into a collaborative document, then delete all of the headings from that text.

2. Instruct students to do an initial reading of the text, highlighting important information.

3. After they finish the text, ask the students to look at their highlights as a way to summarize the information.

4. Have students go back through the text and add in their own headings and subheadings using their highlights.

The goal is not to match the original headings; it is simply to provide an adequate summary of each section of the text.

This is a great strategy for multiple reasons. First of all, it requires students to do more than just scan the text. They have to slow down and identify themes and the gist of each section. This encourages a deeper reading than if the text would have been given with no reading activity assigned with it.

Second, it is a quick assessment tool for teachers. You need only to browse the headings to see if the student has a good understanding of the main ideas of the digital text. In Google Docs, for example, this is even easier. You could just click on the outline view for the document to see a list of the headings along the side like a table of contents.

SQ3R Strategy

The SQ3R strategy is another active reading strategy that I like to use with collaborative documents. SQ3R is a five-step reading strategy that can be applied to both print and digital text:

1. Scan: Scan the document to get an overview of the content.

2. Question: Write down any questions you might have about the content.

3. Read: Read the entire text, using the highlighter and comments features to make annotations and take notes.

4. Review: Review the notes. This would be a good time to have a discussion of the material with peers.

5. Recall: Recall the most important information through reflection or documentation of big ideas and main facts and details.

SQ3R LESSON

For a quick interactive lesson on SQ3R by Mary Burns, visit **bit.ly/ SQ3Rlesson**.

The SQ3R method can be applied for adult learners in professional learning as well. Scan the QR code to see a session I led with our virtual school staff, or read the article about the session and digital reading strategies at **bit.ly/SQ3Rexample**.

Close-Reading and Annotation Prompts

PD SQ3R SESSION

You can also accomplish very simple close-reading activities online. If you copy a digital text into a collaborative document, students could annotate and comment as a whole class, in groups, or individually. This could be done in an open-ended way or could be prompted with specific close-reading questions.

I enjoy using the comments feature in a Google Docs document to facilitate group annotation and discussion around an article. Students can converse with each other in an asynchronous way about their thoughts on a digital text. The teacher can then moderate that discussion, asking questions or pushing the conversation further.

CLOSE-READING PROMPTS

For more ideas to help your students dig deeper into text, check out Kristina Smekens' article, "Plan & Ask Text-Dependent Questions" (2019). The article offers many suggestions on crafting close-reading questions and prompts that might help you as you develop active reading activities to go along with digital text. You can find it at **bit.ly/closequestions**.

Active Reading Tools

Several tools are available to help you create opportunities for active reading with digital text. Here are a few of my favorites.

Formative. Formative (**goformative.com**) enables you to upload a PDF or document and create interactive elements with it. For instance, you could upload a digital text, and then add active reading prompts to the document, tracking student progress. There is also a large library of ready-made activities that you can search and use.

InsertLearning. InsertLearning (**insertlearning.com**) allows you to insert content and assessments onto web pages that get pushed out to students. It enables you to transform passive reading online into an interactive experience.

Edpuzzle. Kate Baker (2019) suggests using Edpuzzle (**edpuzzle.com**), an interactive video tool, to create audiobooks of read-alouds with checks for understanding built in.

Top Tech for Digital Annotation. Common Sense Media has compiled a list of the top eighteen tools for digital annotation that are worth checking out. You can find the list at **bit.ly /CSMannotation**.

Choosing Print or Digital Text

In your blended classroom, it will be important to introduce a variety of texts to your students, both print and digital. So how do you decide what should be in print and what should be online? You must think about what the best tool for the job is in each case.

One thing to consider is the goal of the reading. We know from research that readers of digital text are more likely to recall facts and figures as compared to their print-reading peers, whereas digital readers may struggle more with higher levels of comprehension, without additional supports in place. One strategy would be to match text with the types of comprehension activities you will be employing.

When introducing digital materials and wanting to encourage deep reading, be mindful of the active reading strategies you incorporate. We don't have to completely avoid digital text because of its challenges. In fact, it is for this reason we must intentionally teach students the differences between print and online text and create learning opportunities that help students comprehend all text at a deep level.

Katie Muhtaris and Kristin Ziempke (2015), authors of *Amplify*, suggest pairing digital text with analog reading activities and vice versa. If you have students reading online, have them do an active reading strategy that involves paper and pencil or dialogue with a peer. If students are reading a book or other print resource, consider a digital reading response activity.

Ultimately, it is our responsibility to prepare students for modern reading, and that includes all forms of text and media.

Chapter 6 Key Points

In this section, the important takeaways from the chapter are paired with the ISTE Standards for Educators that inform them.

- People are much more likely to skim and scan digital text than print text. (Educator 1c)
- Without changing the way we provide instruction around digital reading, we can expect lower levels of comprehension when reading online versus print. (Educator 1c)

- By writing digital text using highlighted keywords, front-loading vocabulary, limiting ideas to one per paragraph, utilizing bulleted lists, and more, we can design text for the way that we read online. (Educator 1c, 5c)

- To encourage active deep reading online, we must provide opportunities for digital annotation, meaningful reflection, and conversation around text. Many strategies mentioned in this chapter could help accomplish this. (Educator 1a, 1c, 5b, 5c, 7b)

- We have a responsibility to help prepare students to comprehend all text, both print and digital, at a high level. This means we must approach print text and digital text in different ways. (Educator 1a, 1c, 5c)

Reflection

After reading Chapter 6, take some time to consider how its ideas apply within your context using the questions below.

- Were you able to list all the different types of text you read in the past week? What did you notice?

- What types of text are you currently introducing to students? How balanced is the list between print and digital?

- What are some digital formats of text or media that you could begin introducing to students (blogs, infographics, social media, ebooks)?

- What other active reading strategies can you think of that could be used with digital text?

Share your reflections and thoughts online using the hashtag #PerfectBlendBook.

||||||||||||||||||||||||||||||||||||||||||||||||||||

CHAPTER 7

Getting Started with Digital Content Design

By the end of this chapter, you will:

- Understand the pros and cons of adaptive software versus teacher-created content within the blended learning environment

- Reflect on the role of adaptive software in an artfully designed blended classroom

- Rethink lesson design for digital content, moving away from replication of traditional brick-and-mortar practices

- Understand how design theme choices around things like font and color can impact learning

ISTE Standards

This chapter addresses several ISTE Standards for Educators.

2. Leader

Educators seek out opportunities for leadership to support student empowerment and success and to improve teaching and learning. Educators:

b. Advocate for equitable access to educational technology, digital content and learning opportunities to meet the diverse needs of all students.

c. Model for colleagues the identification, exploration, evaluation, curation and adoption of new digital resources and tools for learning.

5. Designer

Educators design authentic, learner-driven activities and environments that recognize and accommodate learner variability. Educators:

c. Explore and apply instructional design principles to create innovative digital learning environments that engage and support learning.

7. Analyst

Educators understand and use data to drive their instruction and support students in achieving their learning goals. Educators:

b. Use technology to design and implement a variety of formative and summative assessments that accommodate learner needs, provide timely feedback to students and inform instruction.

c. Use assessment data to guide progress and communicate with students, parents and education stakeholders to build student self-direction.

What Digital Content to Use

A key component of any blended classroom is the digital content delivered to students. It makes up a cornerstone of a blended lesson. But what digital content should you use? Teachers may choose to design their own digital lessons within a learning management system or by creating HyperDocs. A school or district might have a subscription to adaptive learning software or online courseware that a teacher chooses to use. And maybe a combination of the two makes the most sense for some classrooms. Whichever approach you choose, you can apply it more effectively if you understand why you might want to use adaptive software or why you might be better served by creating your own digital lessons.

There are several pros and cons to each approach (see Table 6.1 for a summary). What works for one school or classroom may not work for another, and that is okay. Much like designing the blended structures for your classroom, there is no universal "right" decision. There are only correct choices for individual situations.

Designing Your Own Content

One of the first benefits of a teacher choosing to build their own digital lessons from scratch is the buy-in and ownership of digital content that occurs in this situation. You can imagine that when you design your own content, you probably have a stronger understanding of the content and can teach and facilitate those digital lessons with greater efficiency. This may not be the case if you are using online materials from a canned online curriculum, especially for the first time.

Additionally, just as two teachers teaching the same course may not teach in the exact same manner, online instruction can vary just as much. Giving yourself the ability to design the online experience yourself honors those differences in instructional styles and allows you to take full ownership of the digital learning experience, which can be very beneficial for students. The kind of flexibility you are afforded when designing digital lessons from scratch is generally unavailable with purchased online lessons.

Cost savings are another reality. Often online learning solutions that can be purchased by a classroom teacher, school, or district are costly. Designing your own content ensures that the benefits of blended learning are not just for those with a budget to purchase software.

Building digital content from scratch may not always be the best solution, however. There is a lot to understand about designing digital content for the way students learn online, and the design process can be a time-consuming one. As you gain more experience designing and curating digital content, the process will likely speed up. That said, I do not want to downplay the amount of time and effort that teachers spend designing high-quality digital lessons.

Lastly, there are limits in the type of design work that can be done when writing digital lessons in-house using your district's learning management system or productivity suite of tools. You are likely not an elearning designer by trade. Although many tools exist to help in designing dynamic content, content will likely appear more professional and have more features when purchased from a for-profit course or software provider because of the availability of trained staff to do the development work.

Using Purchased Digital Content

If you want to use the most dynamic content, using purchased online courseware could be the best option. Companies selling online software will have developers on staff who can create professional, dynamic content. Online instructional content that is purchased is more likely to have all the enhancements and extras that are not quite as feasible in teacher-created and curated content.

In addition to the professionalism of the content, the responsibility of keeping up with dead links and providing technical support is in the hands of the company and not solely the teacher (although the ability to troubleshoot and be flexible will be important regardless).

As we have discussed, one of the greatest benefits of blended learning is the potential for personalization for each student. One way this can be achieved is through the use of adaptive content. Purchased content created by skilled developers will generally have a greater capacity for this type of sophisticated content. It is far more difficult (but not impossible) for an educator creating do-it-yourself online lessons to build this level of individualization into their digital learning experiences.

Although purchased content can get a blended classroom off the ground quickly, this solution does have some downsides. Teacher flexibility in adjusting the content can be hindered with ready-made online courses or lessons. The ability to add, remove, and edit content and assessments is important when you want to meet the individual needs of each student. If you do not have the ability to modify instruction for students, differentiation and personalization become even more difficult. The levels of customization available vary from product to product, so if purchased content is the route you or your school decide to take, investigating these options will be important. Of course, you will have the greatest level of control over digital lessons you design and build yourself.

Another disadvantage of ready-made content is the standardization that can happen across states. Generally speaking, online content that is created to be sold widely is not always as tightly aligned to individual state standards as what could be created in-house. Taking that a step further, it is even harder to ensure that content that is often inflexible in nature can be adjusted to align closely with a district's or school's established curriculum maps.

Combining Purchased Software and Teacher-Created Content

Of course, in some instances, a combination of teacher-created and purchased content might be the best decision for your blended classroom. As a matter of fact, if you have purchased, adaptive software available to you already, I highly recommend that you take a hybrid approach to designing digital content. You can leverage the adaptive nature of professional content while working it into a teacher-designed digital lesson that is artfully created by the person that knows the students the most.

In general, I recommend thinking about purchased digital software as content within a teacher's designed lesson and not as an all-in-one solution. This helps take the benefits of both types of digital lessons and eliminate some of the cons of working solely with a paid platform.

Table 6.1 Digital Content Options

	PROS	CONS
TEACHER-CREATED DIGITAL CONTENT	• Buy-in and ownership of digital content • Easier to teach and understand content you designed • Honors your unique instructional style • Flexibility • Cost-savings	• Time-consuming • Limited by your technical ability or the tools available to design
PURCHASED DIGITAL CONTENT	• Dynamic, professional content • Technical responsibility falls on company • Adaptive capabilities more often available • Little prep time for you to prepare the content	• Lack of flexibility in many options • Not as tightly aligned to your state, district, or classroom needs • Cost
HYBRID APPROACH TO DIGITAL CONTENT	• Can leverage adaptive content while maintaining flexibility • See the benefits of both types of digital content	• Cost • Purchased content may not integrate directly into the platform that holds teacher-created content

Designing Digital Content

Let's begin to look at what should be addressed and considered when designing digital lessons, whether or not they are paired with adaptive or purchased content. There are several factors that can influence the success or failure of online learning when we design digital materials.

Presentation Matters

To begin, the presentation of our digital content has an impact on how students comprehend the information presented. You probably have shared a similar sentiment to your own students at some point. They could submit work that demonstrates an incredible level of understanding of the material, but if it is not presented well, that message can get lost. The same is true for your online lessons.

Simply introducing digital content into your classroom via blended learning is not transformative in and of itself. William Horton, author of *E-Learning by Design*, said, "unless you get instructional design right, technology can only increase the speed and certainty of failure" (2011). Technology in general is a great amplifier. It can amplify good instruction, but it can also amplify bad practice. The good news is we can design in a way that will improve a student's likelihood of retaining the information shared in our digital lessons.

Consistency of Design

Consistency is the key to beautiful and functional design. If you have ever given students a collaborative activity using a tool like Google Slides, you probably know exactly what happens when consistency is missing. If five students are working on one Slides presentation, that presentation will likely have a minimum of five different themes, a cavalcade of fonts, and an abundance of color—none of which complement each other.

Those kinds of presentations are hard to focus on and generally not very aesthetically pleasing. I like to call these types of slide decks Frankenslides. The same thing can happen to your online lessons when you design each presentation, page, or piece of content separately from the overall design strategy for all of your digital materials. Don't create a monster like this.

Why is this important? We must think about our digital lessons as a second classroom for our students. Generally speaking, we understand the impact of consistency in our brick-and-mortar spaces. You might have a home office set up in your own home. If you do, you probably can attest to the impact of working in a similar space dedicated specifically to productivity. When a student walks into the biology classroom each day, they are a part of the same environment. This is why many schools prefer to have students complete standardized testing in the same place where they learn each day, because consistency of learning environment improves students' testing performance (Houdek, 2018).

If that consistency of environment has an impact on achievement, then what is the implication for our online learning activities? When we design each digital lesson or presentation or document in a way that looks, feels, and operates differently from each other, we are in essence creating a brand new digital classroom with each piece of content. Consider the experience your students have when they "walk into" your digital classroom space each day. Does it feel like the same classroom, or are they having to relearn the space every day?

Don't make Frankenlessons online; consider the elements of consistency that can improve the functionality of your digital materials and your digital learning environment as a whole. You can ensure consistent design if you consider three important things when designing your online activities: navigation, color, and font. I like to think about combining these three elements to create my digital content "brand" and to keep that consistency in all of the learning experiences I create online.

Digital Navigation

Your digital content should be organized in the same way so students know how to move from one lesson to the next every time they jump online. What this looks like will vary based on the platform in which you house your digital content. As you look to design in that space, consider the following:

- How lessons are organized and shared with students
- Where students go to get to lessons each day
- How students navigate and use buttons
- What naming structures lessons use

Creating simple, clean pages with obvious, simple navigation is imperative. Cluttered pages with buttons and icons hidden or inconsistently placed hinder your students' ability to open a lesson and get started immediately. Clear cues for the learner about where to start and where to click, along with plainly labeled buttons, are helpful. It is also a good idea to start your first few lessons with a video demonstrating the navigation. When you create icons or buttons, using the same icons throughout your lessons and placing them in the same location on each page will build familiarity and help with creating consistent navigation.

If you're in doubt, err on the side of providing more clarity. It is almost impossible for you to make navigation too obvious in your digital content. The intuitiveness of the navigation is one of the first impressions you give any person who views your digital lessons. A well organized, easy-to-navigate lesson will allow your students to start a lesson with confidence instead of frustration.

Reflecting on your own digital learning environment, what other navigation considerations would you add to this list?

Use of Color

When choosing colors for your digital content, a good guideline is to use no more than three. These three are the colors that will be used primarily throughout your digital materials. Consider this use of color as part of your online classroom brand.

On a related note, the use of colored fonts should be very limited. All instructional text in your online lessons should be black on a white background. You may have students with vision impairments that would benefit from white text on a dark background, but for the majority of your learners, black font will be the easiest to read. Colored fonts are difficult to read on a screen, especially if you are asking students to do any amount of sustained reading. (Chapter 10 takes a deeper look at how color choices impact the accessibility of digital content.)

Font Selection

Continuity in font selection is another aspect of design consistency that helps students navigate content efficiently and easily find the information they need. When planning out your digital content brand, use the same one or two fonts throughout the entire design. Two fonts can help you create hierarchies that are useful for students, but any more than that can be too much. These fonts should be easy to read. Most people choose a sans serif font for web design. Keep the script, ornate, and novelty fonts to an absolute minimum.

Tools for Choosing Colors and Fonts for Your Digital Content

If the task of pairing colors and fonts for maximum effectiveness seems daunting, help is just a click away. Several online tools enable you to test out your design ideas and provide pairing suggestions.

 Adobe Color. Adobe Color (**color.adobe.com**) can help you select color palettes for your elearning designs. You can use it to find complementary colors, explore existing palettes, or extract color combinations from images you upload.

 **Canva Color Tools.** The maker of the image creation and editing tool Canva offers great resources for color selection on its website (**bit.ly/colorcanva**). The tools include a color palette exploration tool, a color palette generator, and information about the meanings behind colors to help you select colors that send a specific message.

 **Fontjoy.** Fontjoy (**fontjoy.com**) is a simple tool that enables you to generate and explore font pairings to choose the right combination for your digital content.

 Canva Font Combinations. Canva also offers an online font tool (**canva.com/font-combinations**) that is simple to use. You select a starting font, and the Canva Font Combinations tool presents you with font combinations that complement your selection.

Consistency in type size can be helpful in ensuring readability. Sizes in the 12- to 16-point range are most common for elearning content. Anything below that (but especially anything below 10) should not be used online.

Additionally, consistent text alignment is important. You might be tempted to center text on a page, but if it's anything but a heading, centered text for sustained reading is really difficult for our eyes to track and read. Keep all blocks of text left-aligned for maximum readability.

Lesson Design in Online Learning

Design is not only about looks, or as Steve Jobs said, design is "not just what it looks like and feels like. Design is how it works" (Walker, 2003). We can make design decisions that help make our instructional content function better (as well as look nicer). To do so, however, we may have to design for online learning differently than we would for a traditional classroom experience. As you remember from Chapter 6, we interact with online materials in different ways than we interact with print materials or more traditional in-person learning.

That said, it is also important to note that some things are just good teaching regardless of environment. We are not going to throw out good practice simply because we are moving online. However, some things certainly need to be given specific attention and creativity to make best use of the online learning environment.

Gradual Release of Responsibility and Formative Assessment

It is easy to fall into the trap of creating online lessons that are a series of slideshows or videos followed by quizzes or other forms of summative assessment. It is important to design our digital lessons in such a way that the teacher has an opportunity to identify a student's understanding *before* the summative assessment.

When taking a look at your digital lessons, consider how you are designing each lesson to gradually release responsibility to students. Presentations, text, and video are all great modalities to deliver content. However, we should allow students some time to practice or learn the material in a more hands-on way before being given a final grade.

Quick Win: Learning Objectives

It is a great idea to start each lesson with the learning objectives for students. We know if used correctly that focused attention and understanding of a lesson's objectives can mean academic gains and more student ownership (Everette, 2017; University of Colorado, 2007).

When most people begin to share learning objectives in elearning content, they format it in a bulleted list. However, simply writing a bulleted list of objectives at the beginning of a lesson will often result in students skipping over it, as it is not part of the core content. Think about when you post learning objectives on the board or wall of your classroom. Are students independently reflecting on that list each day or does the value come when the teacher intentionally draws their attention to the objectives and discusses them throughout the lesson?

Consider these creative ideas for introducing a lesson:

- Efila Jzar, a high school Spanish teacher, creates comics at the beginning of her lessons to help communicate the lesson objectives. The dialogue between characters draws students' attention. Consider using MakeBeliefsComix (**makebeliefscomix.com**) or Storyboard That (**storyboardthat.com**).

- Some elementary teachers I've visited use a secret agent theme for all of their content, starting their lessons with some dramatic audio that states, "Your mission, should you choose to accept it…" then launches into the learning objectives.

- Health or PE teachers could use a short video or image with speech bubble from a "health and wellness coach."

- James Totton, a virtual school social studies teacher, starts many of his online units with a mandatory phone call or videoconference to discuss the learning objectives and make a plan for the learning. Although his learning objectives are in a bulleted list, the value comes from the conversation with the student where he can draw their attention to it specifically.

To do this, build in practice, short formative assessment, and multiple opportunities for feedback before giving a summative assessment. As Robert Stake, Professor Emeritus of Education at the University of Illinois at Urbana-Champaign, described it, "When the cook tastes the soup, that's formative. When the guests taste the soup, that's summative." (Scriven, 1991). Formative assessment is the true tool we can use to guide instruction (Figure 7.1).

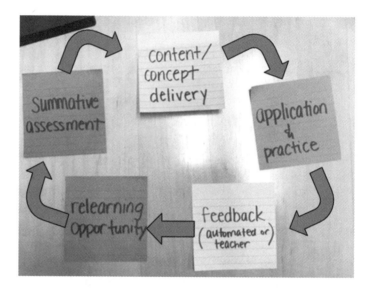

7.1 As you design your lessons, consider how you are delivering the content and then moving through a cycle of formative assessment and instruction before giving a summative assessment.

Not everything a student does in an online lesson needs to be for a grade. As a matter of fact, each lesson does not even require a formal, graded assessment. However, there should always be opportunities for formative assessment present in every digital lesson. In learning, whether online or not, we should always value feedback over a grade. Ultimately, summative assessment should be a small component of your overall assessment strategy within your digital content, much like in a traditional classroom space.

Formative Assessment Strategies

As you are looking for ways to provide formative assessment in your digital content, think about how you can create low-stakes checks for understanding with the goal of learning and improving. These formative assessments should be short and frequent with a focus on learning, not punitive grades.

Probably the first type of assessment many of us think about in online lessons are those that are submitted privately to the teacher to be graded or given feedback by the instructor, often in the form of a quiz or similar assignment. These opportunities for interaction directly with the teacher are critical, as Chapter 9 discusses further. However, there are multiple ways that you can incorporate formative assessment in your digital lessons to improve the learning experience for students and the grading and feedback experience for you.

Self-Reflection

Having students think about their thinking is a great strategy to get an idea of where students are in their understanding of a concept. You can use quick reflection activities to give students a chance to share questions or what they do not quite understand. Reflection activities are short and do not need to take much time, but they can give you a wealth of information. Chapter 8 explores multiple strategies for reflection while examining other benefits of this kind of formative assessment.

Student Interaction

Leveraging the power of peer feedback and assessment can be a helpful formative assessment strategy as well. Getting students to interact with each other can benefit the learning, as learning is social. It also can lighten the load for the teacher, moving some of the feedback responsibility to the students. Check out Chapter 9 for an in-depth look at building opportunities for interaction in your digital lessons, complete with formative assessment ideas to encourage student cooperation and collaboration.

Automated Assessment

Sometimes it is helpful to find opportunities for students to get feedback immediately, without having to wait for the teacher to provide it. Part of building student agency in our classrooms is helping students use their own data to make decisions for their learning. For that reason, using formative assessment or practice tools that generate feedback automatically for students is beneficial.

One way we can do that is through the use of games and simulations. Interactive learning objects and practice games allow students to practice and get automatic feedback on their progress. Plus, using games for this purpose can alleviate some of the stress for students when it comes to assessment. Games are fun and engaging and honestly do not necessarily feel like assessment, so the focus can be on learning and improving.

A Digital Spin on Traditional Assessments

Additionally, you don't have to completely eliminate multiple choice, true/false, or other more traditional assessments in your digital content in exchange for purely authentic assessment. As a matter of fact, I think automatically graded tests and quizzes online can be a powerful learning tool. Now, let me be clear, a digital lesson that uses automatically graded quizzes as the *only* form of assessment is probably not a good idea. If students can Google all of the answers to your quizzes, how can you be sure they are learning the material? We also know that multiple-choice quizzes are not a good gauge of mastery for all learning objectives.

However, I think these automatically graded traditional assessments can be great when they are low-to-no stakes and used by the student as a quick check of their mastery. Instead of using traditional assessments at the end of your lessons to determine proficiency, use them as a tool for student agency. Using short, self-grading surveys or ungraded quizzes can allow students to quickly determine how well they know the information, without having to wait for the teacher to get around to giving them that feedback. Based on their performance and looking at their own data, students could self-select the next piece of content to view and reflect on.

As we have discussed, blended learning and, in turn, the online lessons we give students are most powerful because of the data we can glean from them to make better use of our face-to-face time with students. Formative assessment is one of the key elements that make this possible.

Chapter 7 Key Points

In this section, the important takeaways from the chapter are paired with the ISTE Standards for Educators that inform them.

- Designing digital content on your own versus using purchased, adaptive software is a trade-off of pros and cons. Regardless, there are aspects of elearning design that all teachers need to know to create successful digital learning opportunities for students. (Educator 2c)

- Consistency is the key to beautiful and functional elearning design. (Educator 5c)

- To create consistent design, consider the elements of navigation, color, and font. (Educator 2b, 5c)

- When creating your digital brand for your content, choose up to three colors and two fonts to use invariably throughout your digital lessons. (Educator 5c)

- Although some aspects of good teaching should be applied in any environment, whether digital or face-to-face, we must design digital learning in different ways than we design traditional experience. (Educator 5c)

- When evaluating your digital lessons, consider how you are designing each lesson to gradually release responsibility to students. (Educator 5c, 7b, 7c)

Reflection

After reading Chapter 7, take some time to consider how its ideas apply within your context using the questions below.

- What will your digital content strategy be? Will you use teacher-created lessons, purchased software, or a hybrid of both?

- Considering your digital content strategy, how will you address the cons that may be associated with that type of digital material?

- Thinking about the digital learning platform you have available to you (whether it is a learning management system, Google Classroom, website, or something else), what elements of navigation consistency will be important to consider?

- Create your digital brand style guide. What colors, fonts, and font sizes would you want to use in your digital content?

- Map out a digital lesson you have coming up. Identify the aspects of direct instruction, formative assessment, the opportunities for feedback and remediation, and the summative assessment. What is graded and what is not graded? Are there enough opportunities for students to demonstrate mastery before a final grade?

Share your reflections and thoughts online using the hashtag #PerfectBlendBook.

CHAPTER 8

Cognitive Load and Designing Multimedia Content

By the end of this chapter, you will:

- Understand how we can design with cognitive load in mind to ensure maximum retention of content

- Gain strategies for helping students move information from short-term memory to long-term memory when interacting with digital content

- Learn how to best use audio and video content to maximize learning

ISTE Standards

This chapter addresses several ISTE Standards for Educators.

1. Learner

   Educators continually improve their practice by learning from and with others and exploring proven and promising practices that leverage technology to improve student learning. Educators:

   c. Stay current with research that supports improved student learning outcomes, including findings from the learning sciences.

2. Leader

   Educators seek out opportunities for leadership to support student empowerment and success and to improve teaching and learning. Educators:

   c. Model for colleagues the identification, exploration, evaluation, curation and adoption of new digital resources and tools for learning.

5. Designer

   Educators design authentic, learner-driven activities and environments that recognize and accommodate learner variability. Educators:

   b. Design authentic learning activities that align with content area standards and use digital tools and resources to maximize active, deep learning.

   c. Explore and apply instructional design principles to create innovative digital learning environments that engage and support learning.

Cognitive Load

As you are designing digital content, you should always be aware of something called cognitive load. Simply put, *cognitive load* is the effort being used by the working memory. Some cognitive load is good. We want students to wrestle or grapple with information at just the right level, and a certain amount of cognitive effort is necessary for that to happen. Based on his research, Nelson Cowan (2010) determined that young adults can process about three to five items at once. When there is too much information, however, we max out cognitive load, and our brains are unable to effectively and efficiently process the information. Our ability to retain that information drops significantly.

Information must be held in our working memory before it can move to long-term memory. Cognitive Load Theory tells us that as instructional designers, we need to design learning experiences to reduce the load on students' working memory to help them more adequately process information (Sweller, 1988). There are a few things we can do when organizing our digital lessons to help students move information from their working memory to long-term memory.

Selecting and Chunking Information

What we know about cognitive load and our working memories can be problematic and counterintuitive to our best intentions when designing digital content. As you learned in the previous chapter, simple and intuitive navigation is important to the success of online learning. We often associate the number of clicks with the simplicity of the navigation. For that reason, you might be inclined to put as much information as possible in one location. Although this is done with good intentions, the reality is when we create learning objects or web pages with tons of information or varied kinds of content, we are almost guaranteeing our students cannot process it all.

First of all, we should "aggressively delete non-essential content or move it to an optional appendix" (Meachum, 2018). We discussed this idea in part in the previous chapter when thinking specifically about digital text. Although we should not limit the amount of sustained reading we ask of our students, when designing content, it is helpful to consider what is absolutely necessary and what is optional to the learning. Keeping a folder or document available with additional information that a student could explore independently or be directed to for remediation is a great way to provide lots of different types of content without overwhelming the student during the digital lesson.

The way we chunk information for students is critical, too. If we design a lesson with intuitive navigation between learning objects, we can break up content into smaller, more manageable chunks. As a general rule, twenty short digital lessons or learning objects with simple navigation is better than five long ones. This can help students focus on the material at hand and not be visually distracted away from the content.

Along similar lines, even when breaking up information into smaller chunks, it is easier for our brains to process left-aligned text that is in one column and not multiple columns. This is true as long as the one column of information is not too wide on the screen. The entirety of the width of the text should be in your view at one time. If the lines get to be too long, it is harder for our eyes to track, and subsequently takes more effort and uses more cognitive load.

Negative Space

Negative space is the

empty space around

an object.

When we want to make text stand out, our first instinct is usually to bold the words or make them bigger. This is effective, but adding negative space around text can accomplish the same thing, while also:

- Increasing legibility
- Minimizing distractions
- Simply looking better

Ultimately, we are naturally drawn to more minimalistic designs. Paying attention to the amount of negative space on any given screen our students are looking at can help us create a design that is aesthetically and functionally better. This is something I still struggle with; my instinct is to fill every available space on a page. To help remind me of good practice, I taped the following quote to my computer monitor at work:

Perfection is achieved, not when there is nothing more to add, but when there is nothing left to take away.

–ANTOINE DE SAINT-EUPERY

Reflection

Simply chunking information alone is not enough. Breaking a page of several pieces of content into smaller, more manageable chunks helps with cognitive load in part, but in reality, it is still delivering the same amount of content to the student without breaking up that content consumption for them.

In addition to chunking information, getting rid of superfluous and unnecessary content, being thoughtful about the organization of the pages within our digital lessons, and

Reflection Activity Ideas

Sure, you could simply ask students to "write a reflection," but why not get creative with the assignment to help them stretch their brains a bit more. Here are a few ideas:

- **Quick Writes.** Quick Writes or writing bursts are open-ended, short writing prompts. Some examples:

  Write for five minutes about how this text is making you think differently.

  Write for two minutes about some new learning you had watching this video.

  Write for two minutes about what you would do if you were the character in this chapter.

- **Muddiest Point.** Have students share the most difficult or abstract concept from the material. What is it that they do not understand fully? This one is especially helpful for uncovering some opportunities for remediation.

- **One Sentence Summaries.** Have the students summarize the information in one sentence. This is a more difficult task than you would think because it requires students to synthesize information into a concise statement. This information allows you to quickly see if students are grasping the content as intended, or if you need to provide some additional support or reteaching. A variation of the One Sentence Summary would be to have students write a text or tweet summarizing the material. Give them a character count limit, but allow text-speak, emojis, and GIFs.

- **3-2-1.** After viewing the material, have students share 3 takeaways or pieces of new information, 2 questions, and 1 unresolved area or muddiest point. You could create variations of this one, switching out the reflection task for any of those numbers. This reflection activity, along with many others, could be done in video or audio format instead of written.

- **Sketch.** Have students draw to demonstrate what they know, how their learning has changed, to summarize, and so on.

building in opportunities for student reflection can help with cognitive load barriers. When we have students reflect on their learning and themselves, this helps move the learning from short-term to long-term memory. It also gives the brain a much-needed break.

Incorporating the active reading and viewing strategies from Chapter 6 is one way to help students reflect and think deeply about the content in your digital lessons. In addition to this, you should build in several opportunities for reflection throughout your digital lessons. These reflections can be short and not very time-consuming but still provide a quick opportunity for students to think about their learning

Additionally, reflection can be a great opportunity to get students to look away from the screen and grab some scratch paper. We know there is a certain amount of fatigue that we reach when looking at a screen. As a matter of fact, on average we start to experience eye fatigue after about twenty minutes of reading or viewing on a computer or tablet screen. The good news is that simply diverting our eyes away from the screen, to jot something down on a piece of paper for example, helps to reset that twenty-minute timer (Smekens, 2017).

On a somewhat unrelated note, reflection helps combat academic dishonesty, too. For example, although it may be easy to copy an essay from the internet, it is a lot harder to reflect on the writing process of a paper you did not write. These reflections can serve as a quick gauge of comprehension for the teacher to support their instructional efforts before a summative assessment.

Multimedia in Your Elearning Design

High-quality digital lessons include more than just text-based content. As you are putting together the online content for your blended classroom, think about the best ways to use audio, video, and images to enhance the learning.

Audio

Use of audio is a great strategy for adding varied media to your online lessons. Sharing podcasts or simply embedding audio files to support the content can be options for adding multiple modalities to your students' digital learning experience.

Avoid narrating on-screen text word for word, however. There is some interesting research available about using audio in this way. Ruth Clark and Richard Mayer's work from *e-Learning and the Science of Instruction* showed us that using an audio track to read exactly what is on the screen actually reduces comprehension and retention by 79% on average (2011).

Wow! Just think about that number. There is a good explanation for why that happens, though. Our brains process information through all of our senses. When we are viewing graphics or reading text on the screen, we are activating our visual brain channel because we are using our sense of sight. When we are looking at graphics on the screen, we cannot simultaneously and fully read words on the screen and vice versa. Trying to do both overloads our brain's visual channel. However, when we are visually processing images on the screen and listening to spoken words, that information is stickier for our brains, because it is processed by both the visual and verbal channels at the same time without overloading either. There are special circumstances when this redundancy principle does not apply. If processing the spoken information is too difficult for the student (language learners, for example), on-screen text can be beneficial. Additionally, the impact of the redundancy is not as negative if the student has ample time to hear the narration and separately process the visual information or if there are no images or video graphics present.

Another important reason this redundancy creates problems is that, while we are listening to narration of on-screen text, our brains spend too much effort comparing and mentally reconciling the information, looking for inconsistencies instead of working to process and remember the information (Clark & Mayer, 2011). What we can learn from this research is that audio, and all multimedia for that matter, should *complement* text, not simply duplicate it. When using audio, try using it to deliver material, provide supplemental information, or to record yourself directing students' attention to key points in a text.

Video

Videos are a logical addition to elearning lessons as a way to add varied media to your digital content, especially to demonstrate steps or how to do something. With the availability of such video repositories as YouTube and Vimeo, we are inundated with options for instructional material. There are a few things to consider when selecting or creating videos for your digital lessons.

Keep it short. Bite-sized, concise content is always preferable to longer videos. Videos that are less than six minutes long are most likely to hold students' attention and keep the content to a manageable length that students can process (Guo, Kim, & Rubin, 2014).

I also encourage you to create your own videos when possible. It, of course, is a balance between working harder and working smarter, especially knowing there are lots of instructional videos already created and available online. However, your presence in digital content is critical. Those teacher-student relationships are important in all environments,

Video Recording Tools

If you're new to creating videos or just looking for a new tool to make what you're already doing easier, these three can help:

 Loom. Loom (**loom.com**) is a screencasting tool that allows you to record your screen, video from your webcam, or both. Videos can be embedded, downloaded, or linked to for students. Students can watch the videos at different speeds as well.

 WeVideo. WeVideo (**wevideo.com**) is Google's video editing tool. This, or other more fully functioning video editors, can be used for more sophisticated editing of video. It is comprehensive enough to give you lots of features but intuitive enough to use with young students.

 Screencastify. Screencastify (**screencastify.com**) is a free screen-recording tool designed specifically for the Chrome browser. You can use it to record your screen, video from your webcam, or both. Videos are shared via Google Drive or can be automatically uploaded to YouTube.

both brick-and-mortar and online. When possible, an amateur video created by you that includes your voice or face will almost always be better than a professionally produced video narrated by someone the students do not know.

When recording your own videos, planning ahead will save you editing time in the long run. It also helps you stick to the most important learning objectives for the video, making it easier to maintain that two- to five-minute goal time. Storyboarding beforehand or jotting down an outline can be a helpful strategy when it comes time to record.

You should think about creating opportunities for active engagement with videos in much the same way we discussed for text. Just as we want to use strategies to help students read deeply, we should create those same learning experiences with video. Always think about how students are actively engaged with video content.

Images

The Contiguity Principle states that images and words are more effective when used together than when used separately (Clark & Mayer, 2011). While we should chunk information for our students, at the same time it is absolutely okay (and reinforced by research) to keep images and correlating text together for maximum comprehension. For this reason, try incorporating infographics, instructional images, and other visual media alongside the text you give for a digital lesson. As long as the media is helpful in learning the material and not simply a distraction, your students will be more likely to retain the information.

Cammy Bean (2014) coined the term *clicky-clicky bling-bling* in her book *The Accidental Instructional Designer* to describe all of the superfluous, distracting visual media within a design. We know visual media is important. However, if the visual media we choose serves no purpose other than to look pretty, it becomes a distraction and works against our objectives.

Designing with Multimedia First

One strategy you might consider using is to design with visual media first. Design a page using only multimedia (images, infographics, video, audio, embedded content), and then add text at the end and type only what is not explained using the other media. Typically, when we design digital content, our natural instinct is to type everything out. Then we come back and retroactively add in images or videos to break up the text. I know that is how I naturally want to design, and I would bet you do something similar. When we use this strategy, three things happen.

First, we create a lot of redundancy, and our visual media is less likely to be functional. We add text that explains everything, and the multimedia we add is repetitive. We have already discussed the dangers of redundancy in digital lessons. Starting with multimedia helps us use modalities that complement each other.

Second, when we start with visual media, it forces us to be more intentional about choosing media that serves a purpose. When we start with all text, the images we select often serve one purpose—to break up the text visually on the screen. If we start with visual media and multimedia, those components serve an instructional purpose, first and foremost.

Third and finally, this strategy helps us design with multimedia for the way people read and interact online. If the lesson objective for this particular digital unit or lesson is not sustained reading, we can get rid of unnecessary text that contributes to cognitive load. It also eliminates text that students are likely to skim anyway without some additional deep reading strategies accompanying it.

Chapter 8 Key Points

In this section, the important takeaways from the chapter are paired with the ISTE Standards for Educators that inform them.

- Cognitive load is the effort being used by the working memory. When there is too much information, we max out cognitive load, and our brains are unable to effectively and efficiently process the information. (Educator 1c)

- Avoid putting all of a lesson's information on one page, but rather, chunk the information into manageable pieces linked together with simple and intuitive navigation. (Educator 1c, 2c, 5c)

- Negative space is the empty space around an object. Negative space can improve legibility, minimize distractions, and make your content more aesthetically pleasing. (Educator 1c, 5c)

- Building in opportunities for student reflection can help with cognitive load barriers. (Educator 1c, 5b, 5c)

- When adding in multimedia like audio, it is important that the various modalities in your lesson complement but do not perfectly mirror each other. Redundancy in our digital content can create some barriers to learning. (Educator 1c, 2c, 5c)

- Videos should be short and created by you whenever possible. (Educator 1c, 2c, 5c)

- Visual media works better when it accompanies text. All visual media should serve a specific instructional purpose. (Educator 1c, 2c, 5c)

- Try designing visual media first, followed by adding in only the text that is absolutely necessary. (Educator 2c)

Reflection

After reading Chapter 8, take some time to consider how its ideas apply within your context using the questions below.

- What reflection activity strategies do you want to try or have you tried? What other ideas do you have for giving students opportunities to reflect on content?

- What types of multimedia are you comfortable with using? Are there modalities that you want to seek out additional support to use? Who can help you with that?

- Design Challenge: Try designing a lesson or a page using the Visual Media First strategy. What did you notice by doing that?

Share your reflections and thoughts online using the hashtag #PerfectBlendBook.

CHAPTER 9

Designing for Personality and Interaction

By the end of this chapter, you will:

- Have ideas for how you can showcase your own personality and voice in your digital lessons

- Be able to identify opportunities for students to display their personality within the digital activities

- Reflect on how you can create opportunities for student-to-teacher interaction, student-to-student interaction, and student-to-content interaction within online learning experiences

ISTE Standards

This chapter addresses several ISTE Standards for Educators.

3. Citizen

   Educators inspire students to positively contribute to and responsibly participate in the digital world. Educators:

   a. Create experiences for learners to make positive, socially responsible contributions and exhibit empathetic behavior online that build relationships and community.

4. Collaborator

   Educators dedicate time to collaborate with both colleagues and students to improve practice, discover and share resources and ideas, and solve problems. Educators:

   c. Use collaborative tools to expand students' authentic, real-world learning experiences by engaging virtually with experts, teams and students, locally and globally.

5. Designer

   Educators design authentic, learner-driven activities and environments that recognize and accommodate learner variability. Educators:

   a. Use technology to create, adapt and personalize learning experiences that foster independent learning and accommodate learner differences and needs.

   b. Design authentic learning activities that align with content area standards and use digital tools and resources to maximize active, deep learning.

   c. Explore and apply instructional design principles to create innovative digital learning environments that engage and support learning.

6. Facilitator

   Educators facilitate learning with technology to support student achievement of the ISTE Standards for Students. Educators:

   d. Model and nurture creativity and creative expression to communicate ideas, knowledge or connections.

Humanize Your Digital Content

When we do not think about our digital classroom as an extension of our personal brick-and-mortar classroom, we run the risk of letting our online content become boring and bland. Just as you showcase your personality in your traditional classroom, do not be afraid to let your students see the real you online, too. Doing so helps us humanize online learning, and this is critical.

Your Presence and Academic Integrity

As a matter of fact, humanizing your digital content is a key factor in protecting against academic dishonesty. It is a fear I hear often. Many teachers are hesitant about creating digital content or online learning in general because of cheating. We have this thought that cheating is more prevalent in a digital space than it is in a more traditional, face-to-face learning environment. Would you be surprised to hear that commonly held belief is a myth (Beck, 2014)?

It turns out that academic integrity and cheating have a lot more to do with proximity than the environment in which the learning is happening. Picture this: Imagine you are in a classroom with no technology at all. The students are taking a test. Are the students more likely to cheat if you are sitting at your desk checking your email or if you are up walking around the room while they are completing the assessment? The answer seems obvious. It is easier and more likely that students will demonstrate academic dishonesty if the teacher is not present. The problem is not the paper test. It is not even that students are physically sitting next to each other with the ability to pass notes or whisper to each other or look at their neighbor's answers. The closer the teacher is to the learning or the work, the less likely that cheating will occur (Kelley & Bonner, 2005; Burgoon, et al., 2003; George & Carlson, 1999; Rowe, 2004).

In an online environment, it is not too much different. The main difference is that this proximity has less to do with geographical proximity and more to do with how close the teacher feels to the digital learning that is going on. So what does that mean? If the online lesson feels devoid of the instructor, as if it is some generic content that was given to the student,

115

the teacher's proximity to the learning is far. If it is clear that the teacher is present, whether that is in the videos that are shared, the feedback given, or the way in which the teacher inserts their personality and relationships with the students into the digital content, then the digital proximity is close.

Now does that mean you are likely to eliminate all student attempts at cheating? I wish I could say yes. However, just as you are likely to experience student plagiarism or dishonesty occasionally when no technology is used, the same can be said for your digital lessons. Building relationships and getting to know your students and their work will help you identify when that does happen. In the meantime, you can create an environment that encourages academic integrity.

One clear way to do this is to be an active participant in the learning that is happening. We will discuss this later in the chapter. For now, let's think about how designing digital content in a way that honors your personality and the personalities in your classroom can help you create better, more effective online learning.

Using Humor

Just like you have a style of teaching or way of building relationships with students in your traditional classroom, this should be present in your digital lessons, too. When I am teaching students or adults, I try to keep the learning fun. I often use humor to connect with others. So I do the same thing when I design digital lessons for teachers and students. When you look at the content that I create, I would like to think that you can tell immediately who designed that content. My teacher brand shows up in my interactions, face-to-face lessons and training, and in the online learning I create.

If you are like me and like to use humor with your students, then incorporate that into your lessons and communications. The students will appreciate it, and it is a great way to ensure your presence even when you are not physically there. Keep in mind that you should avoid sarcasm at all times, though. Even if you are good at delivering that kind of humor in person, it is too easy to be misinterpreted in an online environment by a student and ultimately could damage the relationship with the student.

Memes

HUMOR IN LEARNING

MEMES PADLET

Memes, or funny images, videos, and GIFs that spread over the internet, can be a simple, fun way to insert some humor into your digital content or communications.

If you would like to learn about how to use memes in your digital materials, check out the article "Use Humor to Improve Student Learning" at Quality Matters (**bit.ly/QMmemes**). Or, just for fun, head on over to the Padlet wall at **padlet.com/michele_eaton/memes**, and share your favorite teaching memes.

Your Interests

Adding your personality into the content you design does not mean you have to become a comedian. Maybe humor is not the tool you use to connect with kids. Perhaps you love animals or superheroes or any number of things that you use to help students get to know you. Include that in your digital content.

There are a few questions you can ask yourself as you design digital content that might help with this:

- What makes my classroom special? Is that present in my digital classroom environment, too?
- How does this lesson make me feel? Do I feel anything other than bored?
- Can I find the teacher in this content? What about my students?

Use Characters for Just-in-Time Information

Another way to add some fun and personality into your digital classroom space is to use characters. Using characters in your online lessons can be a beneficial way to add a bit of storytelling, create some engaging content, and provide just-in-time information for your students. We often use the internet to find information just when we need it, quickly grabbing our phones and doing a search. By creating a character in your elearning content that provides necessary information "just in time," you can try to mirror how we all, including your students, often use the internet.

You can create a Bitmoji, design an avatar, or use stock photos with speech bubbles to help convey information to students (Figure 9.1). Your character does not need to be fancy, but it is a great way to incorporate storytelling into your online design.

9.1 Say hello to my Bitmoji digital avatar. You can design your own using the Bitmoji app on your phone; install the Chrome extension in your browser, and then easily use your avatar to provide just-in-time information to your students.

Digital Lesson Guides

One way to use avatars or characters in your digital lessons is to create guides that appear regularly throughout the digital content.

For example, throughout a health and wellness unit, you might use some stock photos of fitness coaches with speech bubbles to give instructions to students during each lesson.

Another way to accomplish this would be to use a tool like Voki (**voki.com**) to create animated avatars. With Voki, you can choose an avatar or design a custom one, record audio for it, and then play back the avatar moving and speaking the recording. A few teachers in my district use this tool to create digital lesson guides. For a Preparing for College and Careers class, for example, one teacher created a Voki character that serves as the college and career counselor throughout the course (Figure 9.2). Every time the students see this avatar, they know they can click on it for additional information. Likewise, a U.S. History teacher I know put Abraham Lincoln to work, creating an animated avatar of him with Voki to give helpful information to students through various learning activities.

9.2 This avatar serves as a college and career counselor in an Achieve Virtual Education Academy class on preparing for the future.

In Chapter 8, we talked about the benefits of creating your own videos and audio files, specifically, showing your face in the videos you use with students. Keep in mind that characters and avatars, while a fun addition to your digital content, should not replace actual video of you, the teacher. It is important for the real you to be visible in the course.

Opportunities for Student Creativity and Personality

While it is important for the teacher to have a clear presence in online content, that alone is not enough. If all the focus in the content is on the teacher, what does that say about who the learning is for? We need to be intentional about creating opportunities for students to showcase their personalities and be creative while participating in online lessons.

Considering some of the ideas around voice and choice in blended learning is a great first step. Additionally, just like it is important for you as the teacher to be present in video content, allow students the chance to show their face or record audio, too. Tools such as Flipgrid (**info.flipgrid.com**) and Padlet (**padlet.com**) can be great ways to quickly allow students to put a face and a voice to the work that they submit.

Essentially, the key to making student work more personal is to be intentional about building community in the online space in much the same way that you do in your classroom. Although some time for quiet reflection and independent work is great for learning, not all learning should be done in isolation. Online learning that feels isolating or bland or lacks the relational, human side of teaching and learning misses the mark.

Interactive Digital Lessons

And that leads us to one of the best ways to create community, authentic learning experiences, and engaging digital content: interaction. One of the key characteristics that separates high-quality online content from poorly designed digital lessons is the level of interactivity present. Learning is social and active. That does not change just because some of the learning moves online. As a matter of fact, we have to be even more intentional to design these interactive opportunities when we move learning online to avoid the trap of creating isolating online learning experiences.

There are three types of interaction you should consider when designing your digital lessons:

- Student-to-student interaction
- Student-to-teacher interaction
- Student-to-content interaction

Look for all three of these kinds of interaction in every digital lesson that you design or assign to students in your blended classroom.

Student-to-Student Interaction

Student-to-student interaction includes opportunities for students to engage with each other, either synchronously or asynchronously. This can be done online or offline with multiple students working at the same device. For example, if students are working at the same pace through the digital materials, you can create partner or group work in similar ways that you would in your traditional classroom. Collaborative work can be done silently using digital tools or happen physically in the same location.

There are often tools available in most digital learning platforms that allow for discussions to take place. Students can share their work and thoughts, post questions, and learn from their peers by sharing in a discussion board or similar digital space. Along the same lines, I like to constantly be aware of opportunities to make student work transparent. Sharing to a class Padlet wall or discussion board instead of privately submitting an assignment is a way to give students a more authentic audience for their work while simultaneously building community.

Asynchronous Student-to-Student Interaction

Student-to-student interaction can be a challenge if the students are given flexibility over the pace in which they complete the digital content. If students are not paced exactly together, you have to work intentionally and creatively to create opportunities for students to engage with each other. Making work transparent is a great example of how students can benefit from the contributions of others and the community that is developed, even if it is not happening at the same time.

Group note-taking using collaborative online documents or spreadsheets is a great way to build in collaboration opportunities even when students are not working at the same pace.

One of my favorite simple strategies is to create a graphic organizer and have students collaborate to take notes. This can be done easily with a table-based organizer in Google Docs; each student claims a row for their notes. Then they can use the comment feature to interact with others on the document, while benefiting from the notes and reflections of their peers.

Another option is to create daily, weekly, or biweekly collaborative activities that students can complete regardless of what they are working on in the digital content. These activities could focus on overarching themes or skills that benefit all students no matter what individualized content they are working on independently.

Not Everything Needs to Be Online

Ultimately, you may create a blended learning experience that has a lot of collaborative offline activities. In this case, making the online learning portion more independent is not a bad thing. Like I have said previously, the goal in creating a blended classroom is not to perfectly replicate an existing model or what some other teacher has done in their classroom. You have to craft the experience that makes the most sense for your students. As long as students are given meaningful opportunities to work together, that is what matters most.

Student-to-Teacher Interaction

Student-to-teacher interaction should be incorporated through formative and summative feedback, communication, and engagement in public spaces, such as discussion boards and collaborative documents and presentations within your digital content. Remember, teacher presence impacts academic integrity within your online learning. Even more important than your clear presence in the material that is delivered to students, however, is your engagement with the learning and work your students submit.

Feedback

Timely feedback on the learning is key. Students must know that you see and care about the work they submit. Being a facilitator or guide through discussions and leaving comments on collaborative documents are other ways you can be an active participant in the digital learning.

However, giving high-quality, timely feedback can be one of the most demanding, time-consuming, and taxing tasks that a teacher takes on, both online and offline. We often spend a great deal of time leaving feedback all at once at the end of assignments or projects. If we reflect on the summative feedback we leave students, how actionable are those comments for our scholars? Is it feedback to guide learning, or is it feedback to inform why students received a certain grade?

I believe there is a way we can adjust some of our larger assignments or projects to give more useful feedback. The answer is not more feedback; it's moving that feedback throughout a project or assignment to spread it out and provide students an opportunity to use it. You could split a large project into phases, for example. Instead of having a student submit everything at once, have them complete the project in parts. Then you can provide focused feedback on each section. The final product could be putting the pieces together with adjustments made based on your feedback. This eliminates the need for massive amounts of feedback at the end, students are more likely to submit work that meets the criteria set, and you are able to interact with students in ways that improve learning.

Another strategy to improve the student-to-teacher interaction in your digital content while also making the feedback process more manageable is to use audio or video feedback. That personal touch can truly humanize the online learning experience, which is powerful. It also is a very efficient form of feedback, as you can say a lot more talking than you can in the same amount of time typing.

Student-to-Content Interaction

Student-to-content interaction happens when students are actively engaged in content, either with interactive content or by reflecting on or responding to content. There are two ways you can incorporate student-to-content interaction in your online lessons. You can add content that is interactive by nature or provide opportunities for students to engage with static content.

Content like games, simulations, and learning objects that require students to actively click and participate are examples of student-to-content interaction. These learning objects and activities are designed to be highly interactive for students, and they can be a great addition to your digital content.

Tools to Make Your Content Interactive

Here are some great design tools that can help you create interactive content for your blended classroom:

ThingLink. ThingLink (**thinglink.com/edu**) enables you to create your own interactive content. Simply upload an image (that you have created or found), add icons to it, and link the icons to content you want to display when students hover over the button. You can add pop-ups of text, images, links, videos, audio recordings, and more. ThingLink generates code automatically, so you can easily add the interactive image directly to your web page or learning management system.

Googlink. Using Google Drawings, you can also create interactive images that provide supplemental text, images, videos, and more when students click an icon. Eric Curts (@ericcurts) pioneered the idea of "Googlinks" and wrote an excellent blog post on how to create them. You can read "Googlink: Creating Interactive Posters with Google Drawings" at **bit.ly/ECgooglink**.

H5P. H5P (**h5p.org**) is an open source community of interactive learning objects created using HTML5 (meaning they will work on mobile devices and Chromebooks). This website allows you to enter your own text and images, and grab the automatically generated source code to embed interactive, professional-looking resources into your classes (Figure 9.3).

9.3 An accordion learning object that I created with the help of H5P to use for professional learning

H5P offers templates for creating interactive videos, hot spot images, page layouts, matching games, and more. There is even a personality quiz generator, which you could use to create a hook for a novel study. Students could take the quiz to find out which character from the book they are most like.

Edpuzzle. Edpuzzle (**edpuzzle.com**) enables you to create interactive videos. Via Edpuzzle you can find a video from its YouTube, Khan Academy, National Geographic channels or upload your own. As you then play the video, Edpuzzle enables you to pause it to add assessment questions, your own audio or text notes, or commands to prohibit students from skipping ahead. Later, you can review all the student viewing and answer data from your dashboard at Eduzzle's website.

Open Educational Resources Webmix. On the Symbaloo page at **symbaloo.com/mix/oers4**, you'll find a visual bookmark collection of open educational resources that was originally organized by Kim Hendrick of Indiana Online Academy (@evolvewithkim). I remixed it to add in some of my favorite resources for adding interactive content. Many of the resources bookmarked are interactive; all are curated specifically for educational use; and all are free to use with your students. I have found using this webmix to be a lot more efficient while designing digital lessons than trying to sift through Google, Pinterest, or Teachers Pay Teachers for content with limited success.

DESIGN TOOLS PADLET

Know of a great tool that would benefit your fellow readers? Use the following Padlet at **padlet.com/michele_eaton/designtools** to share your favorite design tools and find a few that others have contributed as well.

Sometimes you may want to use static content in your online lessons, like video, text, or websites. These are resources that the student would use to simply consume information. A good idea when using this type of material is to create some short activity with each resource to add in interactivity after viewing or reading. The active reading strategies shared in Chapter 6 are great examples of this type of student-to-content interaction.

Some other ideas to help create interaction with static content are:

THEY SAY, I SAY

- Collaborative notes templates like the They Say, I Say graphic organizers at **bit.ly/graphorgsearch** (Figure 9.4)

- Reflection activities (see Chapter 8)

- Short self-check formative assessments

- Dialogue with another student

9.4 This is an example of the They Say, I Say collaborative notes strategy. Teachers in my district completed this table as they read chapters from *Empower* by John Spencer and A.J. Juliani and *The Innovator's Mindset* by George Couros.

Foreword - Chapter 2 - Active Reading

Name	They Say *What are some points or quotes from the reading that caught your attention? Some big ideas?*	I Say *What are your thoughts about the ideas? Application to the classroom?*
Meagan C	"Freedom is actually a bigger game than power. Power is all about what you can control. Freedom is about what you can unleash." "Would I want to be a learner in my own classroom?"	One of the biggest epiphanies that I had as I progressed as a teacher was that when I gave students opportunities to decide how they wanted to show their learning or even what direction they wanted to take their learning, they often came up with ideas that far surpassed the complexity of something I might have asked them to do. This taught me two things: 1. Students care more about their work when it is meaningful to them and 2. To always keep looking for ways to provide choice in learning.
Megan G	• "Our job is not to prepare students for something, our job is to help students prepare themselves for anything" • "Every child in your class is someone else's whole world. Empowering students transforms our social/human connections." • "The only thing you can prepare students for is an unpredictable world." • "We must step aside as the gatekeepers and	• This statement is so true and really aligns with our mission in Wayne [as well as my personal educational philosophy]. We are preparing students not only to be great learners within our schools, but also how to be good citizens and transfer their learning as they grow. • This stood out to me because it

Constructive Feedback

As you continue to design digital content for your students, seek feedback on your designs early and often. Even the most experienced instructional designers should get constructive feedback on the digital content they create. Let's face it: Being unbiased about our own designs can be very difficult. Everything makes sense and seems intuitive when it comes from your own mind. If you are designing on your own, reach out to a peer, a friend, or a student for some honest feedback. It will only improve the quality of your work and, ultimately, the academic achievement of your students.

Chapter 9 Key Points

In this section, the important takeaways from the chapter are paired with the ISTE Standards for Educators that inform them.

- Just as you showcase your personality in your traditional classroom, do not be afraid to let your students see the real you online, too. (Educator 5c, 6d)

- The closer the teacher feels to the learning that is happening (not necessarily physically, but their presence in the digital content), the less likely that cheating is to occur. (Educator 5b, 5c)

- Using characters in your online lessons can be a beneficial way to add a bit of storytelling, create some engaging content, and provide just-in-time information for your students. (Educator 5b, 6d)

- We need to be intentional about creating opportunities for students to showcase their personalities and to be creative while participating in online lessons. (Educator 3a, 5a, 6d)

- You should consider three types of interaction when designing your digital lessons: student-to-student, student-to-teacher, and student-to-content. (Educator 3a, 4c, 5b, 5c)

Reflection

After reading Chapter 9, take some time to consider how its ideas apply within your context using the questions below.

- What makes your classroom or teaching special? How might you incorporate that into your digital content?

- How can you provide opportunities for students to showcase their personalities and creativity in your digital lessons?

- Write a quick outline or flowchart of a potential digital lesson that includes all three types of interaction.

Share your reflections and thoughts online using the hashtag #PerfectBlendBook.

Designing Digital Content for All Learners

By the end of this chapter, you will:

- Know the rationale and legal obligations behind accessible digital content
- Understand the nine elements of accessible digital content

ISTE Standards

This chapter addresses several ISTE Standards for Educators.

2. Leader

   Educators seek out opportunities for leadership to support student empowerment and success and to improve teaching and learning. Educators:

   b. Advocate for equitable access to educational technology, digital content and learning opportunities to meet the diverse needs of all students.

   c. Model for colleagues the identification, exploration, evaluation, curation and adoption of new digital resources and tools for learning.

5. Designer

   Educators design authentic, learner-driven activities and environments that recognize and accommodate learner variability. Educators:

   c. Explore and apply instructional design principles to create innovative digital learning environments that engage and support learning.

What Is Accessibility and Why Is It Important?

As we design digital content for our classroom, we also need to make sure those materials are accessible to all students. According to the organization Be Accessible, "accessibility is all about our ability to engage with, use, participate in, and belong to the world around us" (n.d.). At the heart of it, accessibility is about equity of access and ensuring that all students have a level playing field from the start. We do this by ensuring that all students can interact and engage with our digital content from the beginning.

Not only is it our obligation as teachers to create accessible digital content, it is also the law. The Americans with Disabilities Act and Section 504 of the Rehabilitation Act both give us guidelines about accessibility specifically to meet the needs of students with disabilities. These federal laws state that no student should be denied access to any learning activity. To ensure that students are not discriminated against because of their disability, the law says that content should be readily accessible. Essentially, the laws state that students with disabilities should have equal access to the same opportunities as all students.

Accessibility versus Accommodations

When we make our digital content *accessible*, we are taking a proactive approach. Accessible content is content that most students can engage with immediately, regardless of their unique needs or abilities. On the other hand, *accommodations* involve the changes to content and assessment that we make during instruction that is unique to a student and cannot be addressed proactively.

Designing our digital content to be accessible does not eliminate the need for accommodations for our learners. However, if we only ever rely on accommodations, we create roadblocks and obstacles for students that prevent them from having equitable opportunities for success. We never know when a student with a disability of some kind will be placed in our classes. Taking that a step further, some of our students may have undiagnosed or undisclosed disabilities that we may not know about for some time (or ever). Those students deserve immediate access to the learning materials from day one. If we rely solely on accommodations, these students cannot begin their work immediately, because they have to wait on the adults to update the content so they can access it. This puts students at a disadvantage when they do not have equal access from the start.

When we design with accessibility in mind, we are prepared for any student that walks in our door. Additionally, while we rarely teach the same lesson year in and year out, it is not unreasonable to think you may want to reuse and remix the digital content you design. This is another reason to design for all students now, regardless of who you have in the room this year, so you can be prepared for future classes no matter what.

Design for the Nine

Designing accessible content certainly takes a bit more time than designing without accessibility in mind. However, it is a lot easier to design proactively and accessibly than to reactively "fix" content when a student that cannot engage with your content as-is joins your class. As you read this chapter, consider the differences in workload that it would take to retroactively fix issues with inaccessible design versus designing with all students in mind from the beginning.

While you create digital materials for your students, you should consider the nine elements of accessible content:

- Text formatting
- PDF readability
- Use of color
- Animations and visual effects
- Hyperlinks

- Images
- Math equations
- Keyboard navigation
- Video captions and transcripts

Let's take a look at each element in depth.

Text Formatting

Text is often a dominant aspect of many digital lessons. Inaccessible text can quickly compromise learning if steps are not taken to ensure all students can access this content.

Headings and Styles

Headings provide visual cues to navigate a text. As you are reading this book, for example, you probably are using the headings and subheadings. If you go back in the book to review or reread something you read, you are likely to use them to search for the particular section you are looking for. As you read a website, you may not read the entire page if you are looking for one piece of information. Headings and subheadings are handy for skipping through a text to find specific information.

However, a person who is using a screen-reader on a website or digital text because they have low vision or blindness cannot see that visual cue. They rely on technology to help them navigate the page. It is important to make sure our headings and subheadings can be identified by a screen-reader so a person with impaired vision can navigate the text efficiently.

The problem with this is we cannot simply create headings by making the words bold or larger. Screen-readers do not distinguish normal text from bold or italic text. They don't let the reader know that some text is larger than others. They just read the words. So, in this instance, a student who wanted to go back to the text to find some information for an assessment, for example, would have to listen to the whole text again. They would not have the ability to quickly identify headings to pinpoint specific sections of text.

The simplest way to make headings and subheadings accessible is by applying *styles* to text, which you can do from the Styles menu (sometimes called Paragraph Styles) in your word processor (Figure 10.1). Instead of making a heading stand out manually by changing the font size and formatting, select the style that corresponds to the heading's place in your document's hierarchy (Title, Subtitle, Heading 1, Heading 2, etc.).

10.1 The Styles menu in Google Docs

If you are working in a text box inside a learning management system that does not have style options to structure your heading hierarchy, all is not lost. Often, you can type and style the information correctly in Microsoft Word or Google Docs and paste that text into a text box while still retaining the heading code. One way to test this is to check the source code of the text box after you copy the information over. When headings are styled correctly, tags are added around them (<h1> and </h1> surrounding Heading 1 text, for example). If you see these tags, you know the heading is accessible.

Font Choices

It is important to choose fonts that are easy to read. Making your font choices accessible improves legibility for all users, not just those with vision impairment. Stick with simple fonts that are widely available on all devices. In general, texts with one font (two at most) are the easiest to read. Some fonts were actually designed specifically for the web, such as Verdana,

Tahoma, Trebuchet MS, and Georgia, while others, such as script and novelty fonts, make on-screen reading extremely difficult. Avoid the latter, and also avoid writing sentences in all capital letters. Not only does writing in capitals look like you're yelling, but it is harder to read text written this way.

WEBAIM

If you would like more information about font choices and accessibility, I recommend checking out the WebAIM (Web Accessibility in Mind) resources available at **webaim.org/techniques/fonts**. WebAIM is a non-profit organization that provides expertise, guidelines, and tools for designing accessible digital content.

PDF Readability

Students using screen-readers must also be able to navigate PDF files, and not all PDFs are created equal. Consider a PDF file of a magazine article, for instance. It could either contain scanned images of each page of text, essentially static "pictures" of the pages, or a searchable copy of the article's text. A screen-reader can read a PDF only if it contains searchable text, not a static image of a document.

So how do you know if a PDF contains searchable text and, therefore, is accessible? Try a quick test: Open the PDF and try to highlight the text. If you can highlight individual words, the PDF is likely accessible (Figure 10.2). Another easy test is to use the Find function to search for a word that you see on the screen. If you can find the word using the Find function, then a screen-reader can read those words, too.

PDF readability is a great example of how proactive accessible design is much easier than trying to fix issues later. Imagine you are designing a digital lesson and want to use a particular PDF. If you find that it is inaccessible, you simply don't use it and use an alternative resource instead. If you use an inaccessible PDF in a digital lesson and try to make the lesson accessible later, that is a bigger problem, especially if you have designed assessments that go along with that document. In this instance, you have to either find that exact document in an accessible format, redesign the lesson with a new resource, re-type the information from the PDF, or find another way to convert the PDF to accessible form (see the "Microsoft Office Lens" sidebar). Taking that extra step now could help save you some time and frustration in the future.

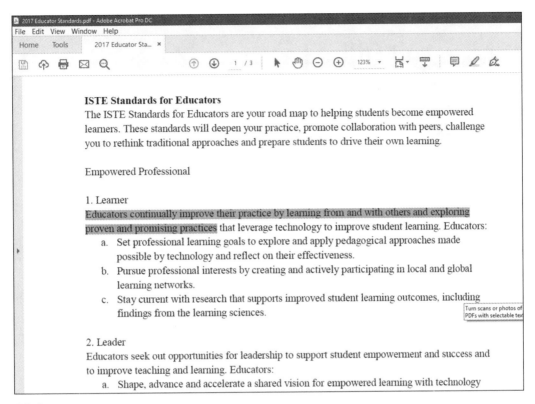

10.2 Because I can highlight individual words and sentences in this PDF of the ISTE Standards for Educators, I know this PDF is accessible.

Use of Color

The way you use color in your digital content can quickly make your online lessons inaccessible if you're not careful. When you design, always consider the contrast between the background and the text, as well as how you use color to indicate action.

Color Contrast

When you add color to your online lessons, be sure to maintain a high contrast between the background and foreground colors you choose. As a general rule, any time students are reading content that is more than a few words, you should use a black font on a white

Microsoft Office Lens

MICROSOFT OFFICE LENS

Microsoft offers a great free tool to help make PDFs accessible. Microsoft Office Lens scans images or PDFs with text, then uses the Microsoft Immersive Reader tool to make the text readable and editable, even if the original PDF is not accessible. For more information, see **bit.ly/officelens**.

background. If you are creating slides or an image with just a few words on it, colored text is okay if there is still a high contrast present, but most text in your digital content should be black. Some students with a vision impairment may benefit from a black background with white text because of the glare a white background produces. This is a case when an accommodation for those students would be the best solution.

WebAIM Contrast Checker

CONTRAST CHECKER

One of the resources on the WebAIM website is the Contrast Checker, which can be a lifesaver when you're choosing colors for presentations, posters, images, and the like. It checks the background color and the foreground color for accessibility and lets you know if your color combinations have a high enough contrast. You can try it at **webaim.org/ resources/contrastchecker**.

EYE DROPPER

To specify a color, you can enter its hexadecimal code in the text box or click the colored box under it to select a color from the color picker. With the help of a third-party eyedropper tool, you can also sample a color from an image, website, or document (I use the Eye Dropper Chrome extension from **bit.ly/eyedropext**). After you enter your colors, Contrast Checker shows you a sample of the combination for normal text and large text, as well as information on whether the combination passes the Web Content Accessibility Guidelines (WCAG) levels of conformance.

For example, Figure 10.3 shows the Contrast Checker in action, evaluating my green fore-ground color for text and navy blue background color. Let me explain what the results mean. The WCAG have three levels of conformance: A, AA, and AAA. Level A is the minimum legal compliance for accessibility, and AAA is the highest level of compliance. (The WCAG contain standards for all of the nine elements in this chapter, plus others.) My green and navy blue combination conforms for both levels for large text but not the AAA level for normal text.

10.3 The WebAIM Contrast Checker tests a combination of two specified colors for conformance with the Web Content Accessibility Guidelines. View the full color image at bit.ly/webaimcc1.

Video accessibility, which we will discuss in detail later, is a great example to showcase how the three WCAG levels build on each other. For a video to be compliant at level A of the guidelines, it must have accurate closed captions. Level AA states that even live video needs to have accurate closed captions and recommends including a transcript of all audio and video. Level AAA includes all of the above plus an additional video of the content being signed in American Sign Language.

It may not always be possible to reach Level AAA of the Web Content Accessibility Guidelines for all of your digital content, and that is okay. When it comes to color usage, though, I generally try to reach the highest level because it is not that difficult to do. The only difference between Level A and Level AAA is a higher contrast between colors.

While Figure 10.3 demonstrates a moderately successful combination that passes for normal text at Level AA and for large text at Level AAA, Figure 10.4 demonstrates what it looks like when the color contrast is too low and fails the checker. Even if you have perfect vision, those colors are hard to look at when together. This is another example of how designing for accessibility benefits everyone.

Contrast Checker

Home > Resources > Contrast Checker

Foreground Color
#FF80C0
Lightness

Background Color
#FFFF00
Lightness

Contrast Ratio
2.14:1
permalink

Normal Text
WCAG AA: **Fail**
WCAG AAA: **Fail**
The five boxing wizards jump quickly.

Large Text
WCAG AA: **Fail**
WCAG AAA: **Fail**
The five boxing wizards jump quickly.

Graphical Objects and User Interface Components
WCAG AA: **Fail**
✓
Text Input

10.4 This pink and yellow combination does not have a high enough contrast to be accessible at any WCAG level. View the full color image at bit.ly/webaimcc2.

Try It with Students

Why not show the Contrast Checker to students, too? If you have ever had students design anything online, I can almost guarantee you have experienced inaccessible color combinations. They are definitely not fun to grade either! Have your students bookmark the WebAIM Contrast Checker on their devices and use it before submitting any work they design. It will be easier for you to view later, but more importantly, it will teach students valuable lessons about accessibility. It is unlikely that students will go through life without creating content for others. It is a valuable skill to learn at any age that we must design for *all* users in mind, not just some.

I have also used this tool with young students. They do not have to understand what WCAG stands for or even about color codes. If they can select colors from a color picker, they can see that green means their colors work together and red means they are too hard to read when paired together. Even our youngest learners can begin to learn about accessibility.

Animations and Visual Effects

Animations and visual effects can liven up your lessons or turn them into an accessibility nightmare.

Flashing Content

Certain animations and visual effects can be detrimental for people with seizure disorders, and because of this the Web Content Accessibility Guidelines state that page content should not contain objects that flash more than three times per second. Personally, instead of trying to count flashes per second, I tend to be a bit more conservative with flashing or blinking content. I avoid it altogether, just to be safe. Ultimately, flashing or blinking on a page is likely to be a distraction from the content we are delivering to students anyway.

As you are directing students to websites, be sure to:

- Remove any flashing or blinking animations.

- Change transitions in presentations to slow, simple animations.

- Avoid using websites with flashing content or ads.

**ADOBE
ACROBAT DC**

What if because you can't find an equivalent resource to offer students, you need to direct them to a web page with flashing content or advertisements? Download the page as a PDF to eliminate the flashing while preserving the content students need. Several Chrome extensions enable you to convert a web page to a PDF, such as Adobe Acrobat DC (**bit.ly/ adobeext**). Many of these extensions allow you to delete aspects of the web page from the PDF, like unwanted ads, for example. When doing so, be sure not to delete information about the website and authors so as not to create confusion about who the content belongs to.

RSS Feeds

RSS feeds on websites are another source of movement and one students must be able to stop. RSS feeds are embedded widgets that can show activity streams on Twitter, Facebook, blogs, and so on; when new posts are made, the feed scrolls through new content. You may have one on your school or classroom website. When sending students to a website that has an RSS feed, make sure all widgets have a pause option. All users should have the option to pause the automatic movement from those feeds. If that is not available, you may want to find a different resource or turn the website into a PDF as described above.

Hyperlinks

You can even create your hyperlinks in a way to be accessible for all users. To do so, be sure the hyperlinked text always describes the contents of the link. Someone using a screen-reader should be able to know exactly what to expect when clicking on a link without reading any contextual information around the link. For that reason, hyperlinking phrases such as *click here* or *this link* are inaccessible and should be avoided. Figure 10.5 shows examples of correct and incorrect ways to hyperlink. The hyperlink should be able to stand alone with no content and the user would still know what they are clicking on.

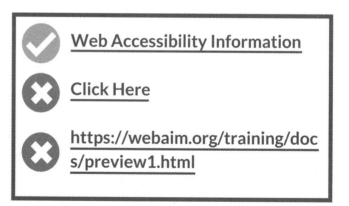

10.5 One accessible hyperlink and two examples of incorrectly hyperlinked text

For a similar reason, it is rarely appropriate to leave a URL as is without hyperlinking to a phrase. Imagine a screen-reader trying to read that third link in Figure 10.5! You will want to avoid using URLs by themselves because a screen-reader will read each individual character listed. That could get really long depending on the URL.

Images

Students who are unable to see the screen have no way of knowing what an image shows unless a screen-reader "reads" it to them. If we are effectively using images in our digital designs, the visual media we choose should have instructional value. For this reason, we have to make these images readable so all students can benefit from them, even if they cannot see them on the screen.

Alt Tags

Any time you use an image, you need to add what are called *alt tags* or *alternative text* to it. Alt tags are descriptive pieces of text that are not visible on the screen but are used by a screen-reader. Students viewing the page without a screen-reader will not see this text. When students access the page with a screen-reader, however, it will read the text listed in the alt tag, describing the image for students.

Although the process for adding an alt tag varies depending on the tool you are using, the tools you need are generally found where you adjust formatting options for the image. Sometimes, you can add alt tags when you initially add or upload an image; learning management systems often offer this option. In Google Slides and Docs, though, you can just right-click an image and select Alt Text from the resulting context menu.

No matter what steps your software requires, the need for descriptive alt tags remains the same. It is worth the investment of time to find how you can add alternative text to ensure that the images you use are accessible to all students.

Longer Image Descriptions

Alt tags are sufficient for short descriptions, but some images may require a longer description than normal. For instance, charts, graphs, and infographics carry a ton of instructional content. For these, you are better off supplying the information in an online collaborative document and adding a descriptive hyperlink to the text version below the image. Essentially you would be creating a transcript of the image.

Please do not let this deter you from using infographics, charts, or tables in your digital content. These types of visual media can be great ways to convey information and make excellent additions to online lessons. As a matter of fact, if you are designing your own

Accessibility on Twitter

Did you know accessibility matters even on social media?

If you are on Twitter or another social media platform that utilizes hashtags, write those hashtags in *camel case* so they can be easily read by a screen-reader. Like humps on a camel, each word of the hashtag should start with a capital letter. A screen-reader would then read #LikeThis as "hashtag like this." Conversely, if a screen-reader encountered the hashtag #notlikethis it would not know where each word began and would have to read each individual letter. Avoid hashtags that are all lowercase.

Do, on the other hand, turn on image descriptions or alt tags for the images you share with your tweets. To turn this feature on (it's off by default), first navigate to Settings and Privacy on Twitter. Select Accessibility and turn on Compose Image Descriptions (Figure 10.6). Now when you tweet, you will see an additional option to add an alt tag to the images you post.

Accessibility

Image descriptions	☑ Compose image descriptions
	Adds the ability to describe images for the visually impaired. Learn more.
Video Tweets	☑ Video autoplay
	Videos will automatically play in timelines across the Twitter website. Regardless of your video autoplay setting, video, GIFs and Vines will always autoplay in Moments. Learn more.

Save changes

10.6 Twitter's Accessibility settings

When you know better, you tweet better.

infographics or images, it can be helpful to plan them out in an online collaborative document. If you create a storyboard or rough plan of the graphic before you begin designing, that document can serve as a transcript of the image later. The planning will help you design efficiently, while serving a dual purpose.

Math Equations

Math and science formulas and equations must be readable by a screen-reader. If an equation is displayed as an image, though, it may not have the proper alt tag to be recognized by a screen-reader. There are three options when creating accessible equations or formulas.

- If equations are saved as an image, add an alt tag to each image with the math equations and symbols typed out in words. Imagine how a screen-reader without an understanding of math might read the formula.

- Use an equation editor tool that has the MathML designation. MathML is an accessible equation writing language.

- Use Microsoft Word documents for worksheets with equations instead of PDFs. Word's equation editor is accessible. Developing equations directly within your learning management system is also a good idea, assuming you can verify that it uses an accessible equation editor within the platform.

Just like with PDFs, if you can highlight individual terms in an equation in your digital content, the equation is likely accessible. On the other hand, if highlighting the equation produces a box around the entire formula, the equation is probably an image that would require an alt tag to be accessible.

Keyboard Navigation

If a student struggles with fine motor movement, using a mouse or trackpad to navigate a website can be next to impossible. For a website or a piece of digital content to be accessible, a person must be able to successfully navigate the page using only the keyboard.

Accessibility Checkers

Several tools are available to help you check your documents and websites for accessibility. You may not need to use a checker on a document that you have designed, as you will know if you added alt tags, used proper headings, selected accessible colors, and so on. However, I do like to use these, especially for content that is shared from other teachers. Before using a document or digital lesson that was designed by someone else, I run it through one of these accessibility checkers to see if there are any issues I need to correct before delivering the material to students:

GRACKLE DOCS

Grackle Docs. Grackle Docs (**grackledocs.com**) is a G Suite add-on that can be used in Google Docs, Slides, or Sheets. Run this add-on while you have the document open to flag any accessibility issues with the text, colors, links, or images. For a short tutorial, check out the video at **bit.ly/grackledocs**.

GRACKLE DOCS TUTORIAL

Microsoft Accessibility Checker. When working with Microsoft products, you can use their built-in accessibility checker. Simply select the Review tab and then choose Check Accessibility to check for accessibility errors and receive recommendations for how to correct them. You can also keep the accessibility checker on while you work, and it will keep you updated about errors in real time.

WAVE   **WAVE EXTENSION**

WAVE Web Accessibility Evaluation Tools. WebAIM offers a group of accessibility checkers called WAVE (**wave.webaim.org**). You can check the accessibility of a link by entering it on the WAVE page of the WebAIM website or install an extension in Chrome or Firefox (**wave.webaim.org/extension**).

To test a website's keyboard navigation accessibility, try:

- Pressing the Tab key to navigate from button to button on a site
- Pressing Shift+Tab to go back to the previous button or link
- Pressing the Spacebar or Enter key while a link is selected to activate that link or button

Fortunately, if you are creating documents in Microsoft Office or G-Suite, you can rest assured that those platforms have accessible navigation. Most popular learning management systems also have platforms that are accessible without the use of a mouse. Navigation accessibility becomes more of a question when you direct students to outside websites. However, it does not take much time at all to check a site before providing the link to students.

Video Captions and Transcripts

As mentioned previously, to be legally compliant and meet Level A requirements under the Web Content Accessibility Guidelines, all pre-recorded videos must have accurate subtitles or a transcript available. These can be manually added or automatically generated, as long as they are accurate. Captioning or transcribing videos will most likely be your most time-consuming task when making sure your digital materials are accessible before delivering them to students.

Although YouTube can automatically generate captions, remember that voice-to-text automation is not perfect. If you are using a YouTube video, check all of the captions for accuracy.

If you upload your own video to YouTube, you can edit the automated captions or create the subtitles yourself. Editing the automatically generated subtitles and just correcting the mistakes is a fairly efficient way to create accurate closed captions. Keep in mind, though, that you have no control over the subtitles in someone else's video. If you are using a video platform where closed captioning is not available or if you are using someone else's video with missing or inaccurate subtitles, you can type a transcript of the video in an online collaborative document and link it below the video.

We discussed in Chapter 8 how creating your own videos can be helpful for your learners as they engage with the digital lessons you develop. Doing this can also save you the time and hassle of transcribing someone else's video. Not only can you edit automatically generated

Google Closed Captioning Tools and Strategies

In addition to the tools built into YouTube, you can also use Google tools to help with various closed-caption and subtitle tasks:

- **Voice to Text in Google Docs.** The Voice Typing tool in Google Docs enables you to create a transcript of a video when you use it strategically. From the Tools menu, choose Voice Typing to turn on the voice-to-text feature, and then play the video you need a transcript of. Google Docs will transcribe what it hears from the video into a document. You can then edit the document to correct any inaccuracies. Using this feature allows you to re-create YouTube's automatically generated and editable closed captions.

- **Real-Time Closed Captioning in Google Slides.** Google Slides now has automated closed captioning that you can use in real time. When you are in Present mode, click the CC option at the bottom and choose your font size. This is great for presentations or lectures using Slides and is *surprisingly accurate*.

- **Live Captions in Google Meet.** Google Meet is Google's videoconferencing tool, and it now supports live captions for online meetings. You can use this if you are meeting with a student or a guest speaker and need to provide subtitles of the conversation.

subtitles with ease, you can also plan ahead to lighten the load. When creating your own video, you could write the transcript before recording. Doing this will help you stay on topic and keep the video concise. You can also then use that script as a linkable transcript after creating the video.

Know Better, Do Better

After reading this chapter, you might be feeling overwhelmed. I know I felt that way when I learned about accessibility. My first thoughts went to all of the content I had created before that I knew was inaccessible. I wanted to immediately fix everything I had ever done, and that feeling caused stress and anxiety. How was I ever going to fix all of that content?

Allow yourself some grace. You may never be able to change everything you have ever created for students. I recommend focusing your attention on the future and the materials you create and curate moving forward.

10.7 The words of poet Dr. Maya Angelou apply to your work with accessible digital content. When we know better, we do better.

> **Maya Angelou** ✔
> @DrMayaAngelou
>
> "Do the best you can until you know better. Then when you know better, do better." #MayaAngelou

Chapter 10 Key Points

In this section, the important takeaways from the chapter are paired with the ISTE Standards for Educators that inform them.

- Accessible content is content that almost all students can engage with immediately, regardless of their unique needs or abilities. On the other hand, accommodations involve the changes to content and assessment that we make during instruction that are unique to a student and cannot be addressed proactively. (Educator 2b)

- It is our responsibility as educators to ensure that the content we deliver to students is accessible, both because of a legal obligation and because it is what is best for our students. (Educator 2b, 2c)

- The nine elements of accessibility to consider for your digital content are: text formatting, PDF readability, color, animations and visual effects, hyperlinks, images, math equations, keyboard navigation, and video captions and transcripts. (Educator 2b, 5c)

- Although you may not have the time to go back and fix all of the digital content you have created up until this point, you can focus on making sure the digital materials you create moving forward are all accessible. (Educator 2b, 2c, 5c)

Reflection

After reading Chapter 10, take some time to consider how its ideas apply within your context using the questions below.

- How accessible are your color combinations? Try out the WebAIM Contrast Checker to test colors you have used in a recent presentation or test the colors of some of your favorite Microsoft PowerPoint or Google Slides themes.

- What are some examples of accessible and inaccessible hyperlinks you've added to your lessons? How would you change them? What examples can you find online?

- How accessible is the navigation for your favorite student websites or even your classroom website? Can you move through the page without the use of a mouse or trackpad?

- What aspects of accessibility could you reasonably teach students about as they create in the classroom?

Share your reflections and thoughts online using the hashtag #PerfectBlendBook.

CHAPTER 11

Taking the First Step and Moving Forward

By the end of this chapter, you will:

- Be ready to take the first step in your blended learning journey

- Recognize good places to start when first implementing blended learning

- Know how to get support to minimize struggle and maximize effort

ISTE Standards

This chapter addresses several ISTE Standards for Educators.

1. Learner

   Educators continually improve their practice by learning from and with others and exploring proven and promising practices that leverage technology to improve student learning. Educators:

   a. Set professional learning goals to explore and apply pedagogical approaches made possible by technology and reflect on their effectiveness.

   b. Pursue professional interests by creating and actively participating in local and global learning networks.

2. Leader

   Educators seek out opportunities for leadership to support student empowerment and success and to improve teaching and learning. Educators:

   a. Shape, advance and accelerate a shared vision for empowered learning with technology by engaging with education stakeholders.

4. Collaborator

   Educators dedicate time to collaborate with both colleagues and students to improve practice, discover and share resources and ideas, and solve problems. Educators:

   a. Dedicate planning time to collaborate with colleagues to create authentic learning experiences that leverage technology.

Take the First Step

We have covered a lot of ground, considering the elements of blended learning in both the physical classroom and the digital classroom. Hopefully, you are feeling inspired, motivated, and empowered to take the next step in transforming your classroom to a more student-centered environment.

But, maybe, too, you feel just a bit overwhelmed by all of the choices and ways that you can find your perfect blend—that is perfectly okay! My own experiences and every other example in this book share one important commonality: The blended learning in each of these class-rooms evolved and changed. We all started somewhere.

For me, my first step was a tiny one. Back in Chapter 1, I spoke about the first time I dipped my toes into blended learning. I started with one independent reading activity, and I moved it online. That one simple change began a ripple effect of activities that led me to where I am today. Although that first step for me was far from noteworthy or transformative, it was important. Once you take that first step, it makes the next step just that much more attainable. Then after that, you can take another step forward.

So I encourage you to choose that first step. Will it be to create a digital lesson for one unit and incorporate it into stations? Maybe you want to try creating a playlist or a checklist for one week of math class. Or maybe your first step is to leverage available resources to give yourself some small group instruction time. Whatever it is, take that step. Then learn from that experience. Most likely, things will not go perfectly according to plan—that is okay, too. Learning is messy for students *and* for teachers. Part of finding the perfect blend for your classroom is taking calculated risks and iterating based on the unique needs that pop up in your class.

Ivan Turgenev, a Russian novelist and poet, said it best: "If we wait for the moment when everything, absolutely everything is ready, we shall never begin" (1877).

Get Support and Move Forward

While your blended journey will not be perfect and you may come across hurdles along the way, you do not have to go it alone. I encourage you to actively seek out a community of educators to share the work with. Hopefully, you are surrounded by teachers in your building who want to tackle this work with you, whether they are teachers on your grade level team, in your department, or just friendly peers who are excited about the possibilities of blended learning. Seek out these partnerships in your building if you can. Developing digital materials and shifting the structures in your classroom can definitely be a worthwhile experience, but it can also involve a lot of effort. Sharing that workload with others can go a long way. As I began blending my own classroom, I was often designing on my own. However, I took any chance I could to collaborate on a lesson with a member of my grade team or to bounce ideas off of an instructional coach in my district. We were better together, and the workload was ultimately lightened.

If, despite your efforts within your physical community, you feel isolated, reach out to the digital community. Remember, you're not in this alone. If you haven't already, check out the hashtag #PerfectBlendBook on Twitter, Instagram, or other social media platforms to share your thoughts and connect with other readers. There are so many people out here ready to connect with you—myself included. Use these platforms to grow your personal learning network, ask questions, share ideas and resources, and be inspired. You can always shoot me a tweet, too, and I would love to connect.

Working alongside and connecting with like-minded educators, whether face-to-face or online, makes all the difference. Together we can minimize the struggle of trying something new and maximize our effectiveness in the classroom.

The Perfect Blend

As you connect with others and revisit the resources and examples from this book, keep in mind that the blended learning experience you craft for your students should be as unique as the learners in your classroom. If we are committed to creating student-centered learning experiences, then our blended learning classrooms should be tailored to them.

My goal is not to have you perfectly replicate a blended learning model or an example from another classroom. Rather, consider each element of a blended learning experience, think about the needs of your students, get input directly from your students, and create a unique experience. Then reflect on it, iterate, and adjust to continue to craft a blended classroom that works for you and your students.

The perfect blend is not a recipe you replicate. The perfect blend is designed from scratch for you and your students' taste.

References

Allyn, P., & Burns, M. (2017). *Taming the wild text: Literacy strategies for today's reader.* Huntington Beach, CA: Shell Education.

Arnett, T. (2018, May 9). The secret element in blended learning [Blog post]. *Clayton Christensen Institute.* Retrieved from **christenseninstitute.org/blog/the-secret-element -in-blended-learning/?_sft_topics=personalized-blended-learning&sf_paged=2**

Baker, K. (2019, March 10). Teaching (digital) literacy: Driving students to the intersection of reading, writing, & discussion [Blog post]. *Baker's BYOD: Documenting the integration of technology and therapy dogs in the high school English classroom.* Retrieved from **kbakerbyodlit .blogspot.com/2019/03/teaching-digital-literacy-driving.html**

Be Accessible. (n.d.). The movement: What is accessibility. Retrieved from **beaccessible .org.nz/the-movement/what-is-accessibility**

Bean, C. (2014). *The accidental instructional designer.* Alexandria, VA: American Society for Training & Development.

Beck, V. (2014). Testing a model to predict online cheating—Much ado about nothing. *Active Learning in Higher Education. 15*(1), 65–75.

Ben-Yehudah, G., & Eshet-Alkalai, Y. (2014, January). The influence of text annotation tools on print and digital reading comprehension. *Proceedings of the 9th Chais Conference for the Study of Innovation and Learning Technologies: Learning in the Technological Era.* Retrieved from **researchgate.net/publication/312549391_The_influence_of_text_annotation _tools_on_print_and_digital_reading_comprehension**

Bjerede, M. (2018, May 22). What counts as student agency? *Getting Smart.* Retrieved from **gettingsmart.com/2018/05/what-counts-as-student-agency**

Bray, B. (2019, August 16). Getting to know you with your learner profile. *Rethinking Learning.* Retrieved from **barbarabray.net/2019/08/16/getting-to-know-you-with -your-learner-profile**

Bray, B., & McClaskey, K. (2016). *How to personalize learning: A practical guide for getting started and going deeper.* Thousand Oaks, CA: Corwin.

Burgoon, J., Stoner, M., Bonita, J., & Dunbar, N. (2003, January). Trust and deception in mediated communication. *36th Hawaii International Conference on Systems Sciences*, 44a.

Clark, R. C., & Mayer, R. E. (2011). *E-learning and the science of instruction, 3rd edition.* San Francisco, CA: Pfeiffer.

Clayton Christensen Institute. (2019). Blended Learning Models. *Blended Learning Universe.* Retrieved from **blendedlearning.org/models**

Coiro, J. (2011, October 12). Predicting reading comprehension on the Internet: Contributions of offline reading skills, online reading skills, and prior knowledge. *Journal of Literacy Research.* Retrieved from **journals.sagepub.com/doi/full/10.1177/1086296x11421979**

Common Sense Media. (n.d.). Top tech for digital annotation. Retrieved from **commonsense.org/education/top-picks/top-tech-for-digital-annotation**

Cowan, N. (2010, February 1). The magical mystery four: How is working memory capacity limited, and why? *Current Directions in Psychological Science, 19*(1), 51–57. Retrieved from **ncbi.nlm.nih.gov/pmc/articles/PMC2864034**

Curts, E. (2016, May 16). Googlink: Creating interactive posters with Google Drawings [Blog post]. *Control Alt Achieve.* Retrieved from **controlaltachieve.com/2016/05/googlink-google-drawings-thinglink.html**

Everette, M. (2017, October 18). The hidden power of learning objectives [Blog post]. *Scholastic.* Retrieved from **scholastic.com/teachers/blog-posts/meghan-everette/17-18/The-Hidden-Power-of-Learning-Objectives**

Fried, R. (2005). *The game of school: Why we all play it, how it hurts kids, and what it will take to change it.* San Francisco, CA: Jossey-Bass.

Garrison, R., & Kanuka, H. (2004, February 13). Blended learning: Uncovering its transformative potential in higher education. *The Internet and Higher Education, 7,* 95–105. Retrieved from **click4it.org/images/5/58/Garrison,_Kanuka.pdf**

Garrison, R., & Vaughan, H. (2008). *Blended learning in higher education: Framework, principles and guidelines.* San Francisco, CA: Jossey-Bass.

George, J., & Carlson, J. (1999, January). Group support systems and deceptive communication. *Speech presented at 32nd Hawaii International Conference on System Sciences.*

Gerbic, P. (2006). On-campus students' learning in asynchronous environments. *Unpublished doctoral thesis*, Deakin University, Melbourne, Australia.

Gonzalez, J. (2017, June 11). How HyperDocs can transform your teaching. *Cult of Pedagogy*. Retrieved from **cultofpedagogy.com/hyperdocs**

Gonzalez, J. (2018, March 18). 12 ways to upgrade your classroom design. *Cult of Pedagogy*. Retrieved from **cultofpedagogy.com/upgrade-classroom-design**

Guo, P. J., Kim, J., & Rubin, R. (2014). How video production affects student engagement: An empirical study of MOOC videos. Retrieved from **up.csail.mit.edu/other-pubs /las2014-pguo-engagement.pdf**

Haile, T. (2014, March 9). What you think you know about the web is wrong. *Time Magazine*. Retrieved from **time.com/12933/what-you-think-you-know-about-the-web-is-wrong**

Hare, R. L., & Dillon, R. (2016). *The space: A guide for educators.* Irvine, CA: EdTechTeam Press.

Hendrick, K. (n.d.). IOA OERs. Retrieved from **symbaloo.com/mix/oers5**

Higgins, S., Kokotsaki, D., & Coe, R. (2012, July). The teaching and learning toolkit. Retrieved from **lancsngfl.ac.uk/secondary/seniorleaders/download/file/SUTTON TRUST T&L toolkit July 2012.pdf**

Horn, M., & Staker, H. (2015). *Blended: Using disruptive innovation to improve schools.* San Francisco, CA: Jossey-Bass.

Horton, W. (2011). *E-Learning by design.* San Francisco, CA: Pfeiffer.

Houdek, K. (2018, March). Efficient vs. effective environments: Testing the testing environment: Where students take a test can make a difference in their ability to perform. *Association for Middle Level Education*. Retrieved from **amle.org/BrowsebyTopic /WhatsNew/WNDet/TabId/270/ArtMID/888/ArticleID/904/Efficient-vs-Effective -Environments-Testing-the-Testing-Environment.aspx**

International Society for Technology in Education. (2017). *ISTE Standards for Educators*. Retrieved from iste.org/standards/for-educators

Iyengar, S., & Lepper, M. (2000, June 19). When choice is demotivating: Can one desire too much of a good thing? *Personality Processes and Individual Differences*. Retrieved from **faculty.washington.edu/jdb/345/345 Articles/Iyengar %26 Lepper (2000).pdf**

Julian, S. (2018). Digital texts and reading strategies. *ACRL Tips and Trends: Instructional Technologies Committee.* Retrieved from **acrl.ala.org/IS/wp-content/uploads/Tips-and -Trends-Spl8.pdf**

Kaufman, G., & Flanagan, M. (2016, May). High-low split: Divergent cognitive construal levels triggered by digital and non-digital platforms. *CHI '16 Proceedings of the 2016 CHI Conference on Human Factors in Computing Systems.* Retrieved from **dl.acm.org/citation .cfm?doid=2858036.2858550**

Kelley, K., & Bonner, K. (2005). Digital text. Distance education and academic dishonesty: Faculty and administrator perception and responses. *Journal of Asynchronous Learning Network*, 9, 43–52.

Kish, M., & Kish, J. (2017, March 14). Blended learning student checklist [Blog post]. *DSD Professional Development.* Retrieved from **dsdprofessionaldevelopment.com/ blended-learning-blog/blended-learning-student-checklist**

Kish, M., & Kish, J. (2017, May 11). Garage sale choice board activities [Blog post]. *DSD Professional Development.* Retrieved from **dsdprofessionaldevelopment.com/ blended-learning-blog/garage-sale-choice-board-activities**

Konnikova, M. (2014, July 16). Being a better online reader. *The New Yorker.* Retrieved from **newyorker.com/science/maria-konnikova/being-a-better-online-reader**

Korbey, H. (2018, August 21). Digital text is changing how kids read—Just not in the way that you think. *Mindshift.* Retrieved from **kqed.org/mindshift/49092/digital -text-is-changing-how-kids-read-just-not-in-the-way-that-you-think**

Leap Innovations. (2019). Entrance tickets to drive learning plans. Retrieved from **leapinnovations.org/resource/entrance-tickets-to-drive-learning-plans**

Meacham, M. (2018, November 6). TMI! Cognitive overload and learning. *LearningToGo.* Retrieved from **learningtogo.info/2018/11/tmi-cognitive-overload-and-learning-2**

Miller, C. C., & Bosman, J. (2011, May 19). E-books outsell print books at Amazon. *New York Times.* Retrieved from **nytimes.com/2011/05/20/technology/20amazon.html**

Mochon, D. (2013). Single-option aversion. *Journal of Consumer Research. 40* (October), 555–566.

Moore, A. (2019). Interviewed by Michele Eaton.

Morris, S. (n.d.). Secondary (MS/HS) playlist. *Choice Boards and Playlists.* Retrieved from **sites.google.com/rusdlearns.net/choice-boards-and-playlists/secondary-mshs -playlists?authuser=0**

Mueller, D. (2019, March 4). Three ways to blend and personalize your classroom [Blog post]. *TeacherVision.* Retrieved from **teachervision.com/blog/morning-announcements /three-ways-to-blend-and-personalize-your-classroom**

Muhtaris, K., & Ziemke, K. (2015). *Amplify: Digital teaching and learning in the K–6 classroom.* Portsmouth, NH: Heinemann.

Nielsen, J. (1997, September 30). How users read on the web. *Nielsen Norman Group.* Retrieved from **nngroup.com/articles/how-users-read-on-the-web**

Olszewski-Kubilius, P. (2013, May 20). Setting the record straight on ability grouping. *Education Week.* Retrieved from **edweek.org/tm/articles/2013/05/20/fp_olszewski.html**

Patnoudes, E. (2017, November). 7 tips for redesigning your learning space. *EdTech Focus on K–12.* Retrieved from **edtechmagazine.com/k12/article/2017/11/7-tips-redesigning -your-learning-space**

Puzio, K., & Colby, G. (2010). The effects of within class grouping on reading achievement: A meta-analytic synthesis. *Society for Research on Educational Effectiveness.* Retrieved from **eric.ed.gov/?id=ED514135**

Reading Horizons. (2019). The Rotation Model. Retrieved from **readinghorizons.com /literacy-articles/blended-reading-approach/models/rotation-model**

Ross, B., Pechenkina, E., Aeschliman, C., & Chase, A. (2017, November 3). Print versus digital texts: Understanding the experimental research and challenging the dichotomies. *Research in Learning Technology.* Retrieved from **journal.alt.ac.uk/index.php/rlt/article /view/1976/2193**

Rowe, N. (2004). Cheating in online student assessment: Beyond plagiarism. *Online Journal of Distance Learning.* Retrieved from **westga.edu/~distance/ojdla/summer72/rowe72.html**

Scalzetti, C. (2019). Interviewed by Michele Eaton.

Schwartz, K. (2016, October 16). Strategies to help students 'go deep' when reading digitally. *Mindshift.* Retrieved from **kqed.org/mindshift/46426/strategies-to-help -students-go-deep-when-reading-digitally**

Scriven, M. (1991). *Evaluation thesaurus.* Newbury Park, CA: SAGE Publications, Inc.

Smekens, K. (2017, March 10). Maximize on-screen reading time. *Smekens Education Solutions.* Retrieved from **smekenseducation.com/Maximize-On-Screen-Reading-Time.html**

Smekens, K. (2019, March 1). Plan & ask text-dependent questions. *Smekens Education Solutions.* Retrieved from **smekenseducation.com/Plan-Ask-TextDependent-Question0.html**

Stacey, E., & Gerbic, P. (2008, January). Success factors for blended learning. Retrieved from **researchgate.net/publication/228402600_Success_factors_for_blended_learning**

Subrahmanyam, K., Michikyan, M., Clemmons, C., Carrillo, R., Uhls, Y., & Greenfield, P. (2013). Learning from paper, learning from screens: Impact of screen reading and multi-tasking conditions on reading and writing among college students. *International Journal of Cyber Behavior, Psychology and Learning, 3*(4), 1–27. Retrieved from **pdfs.semanticscholar.org/b951/edbf5df08aa2366c575c246bc32ceae3l044.pdf**

Sweller, J. (1988, April). Cognitive load during problem solving: Effects on learning. *Cognitive Science: A Multidisciplinary Journal.* Retrieved from **onlinelibrary.wiley.com/doi/abs/10.1207/s15516709cog1202_4**

Taylor, M. (n.d.). Redundancy principle: Should you duplicate narrated text on-screen? *E-Learning Heroes.* Retrieved from **community.articulate.com/articles/redundancy-principle-should-you-duplicate-narrated-text-on-screen**

The Learning Accelerator (n.d.). Lindsay High School. *Blended & personalized learning at work: See schools in action.* Retrieved from **practices.learningaccelerator.org/see/lindsay-high-school**

The Learning Accelerator (n.d.). Pleasant View Elementary School. *Blended & personalized learning at work: See schools in action.* Retrieved from **practices.learningaccelerator.org/see/pves**

Turgenev, I. (2009). *Virgin soil [1877].* Ithaca, NY: Cornell University Library.

University of Colorado. (2007). Module 3: Learning objectives. *Assessment & Instructional Alignment: An Online Tutorial for Faculty.* Retrieved from **ucdenver.edu/faculty_staff/faculty/center-for-faculty-development/Documents/tutorials/Assessment/module3/index.htm**

U.S. Department of Education. (n.d.). Protecting students with disabilities. *Office for Civil Rights.* Retrieved from **www2.ed.gov/about/offices/list/ocr/504faq.html?exp=0**

U.S. Department of Justice Civil Rights Division. (n.d.). Information and technical assistance on the Americans with Disabilities Act. Retrieved from **ada.gov**

Walker, R. (2003, November 30). The guts of a new machine. *The New York Times Magazine*. Retrieved from **nytimes.com/2003/11/30/magazine/the-guts-of-a-new-machine.html**

WebAIM. (n.d.). Fonts. Retrieved from **webaim.org/techniques/fonts**

WebAIM. (n.d.). Web Content Accessibility Guidelines. Retrieved from **webaim.org /standards/wcag**

White, J. (2017, September 12). Figuring out flexibility in an elementary classroom [Blog post]. *Clayton Christensen Institute*. Retrieved from **christenseninstitute.org/blog /figuring-flexibility-elementary-classroom**

Wolf, M. (2018, August 25). Skim reading is the new normal. The effect on society is profound. *The Guardian*. Retrieved from **theguardian.com/commentisfree/2018/aug /25/skim-reading-new-normal-maryanne-wolf**

Wolf, M. (2019). *Reader, come home: The reading brain in a digital world*. New York City, NY: Harper Paperbacks.

Young, C. (2020). Interviewed by Michele Eaton.

Index